BET

THE WHITE
LINES

COACH W.T. JOHNSTON'S
DETERMINED PURSUIT OF *ULTIMATE VICTORY*

DAVE BURCHETT

Between the White Lines

Coach W.T. Johnston's Determined Pursuit of Ultimate Victory
Copyright © 2019 by Dave Burchett

Printed in the United States of America

ISBN 978-0-578-22330-8

CONTENTS

God's definition of success is really one of significance—the significant difference our lives can make in the lives of others. This significance doesn't show up in win-loss records, long résumés, or the trophies gathering dust on our mantels. It's found in the hearts and lives of those we've come across who are in some way better because of the way we lived.

— Tony Dungy

FOREWORD

I have worked in sports all my life, primarily producing and directing live television sports. I have participated in upward of five thousand live telecasts over four decades. I have hung around a lot of famous and infamous coaches over that span. I have met enough coaches to become immune to and a little cynical about the "coach speak" you hear before big games.

I first heard about W.T. Johnston during the 2014 Texas high school football season. I was aware of the adversity he had faced, but his story fell off my radar after the season. I reconnected with W.T. during the 2017 season and became intimately aware of his journey. We became friends, and I became convinced that his remarkable story needed to be told.

You don't meet too many extraordinary people in this life. W.T. Johnston is one of them. It is my absolute privilege to tell you his story.

1

GROWING UP SOUTHERN

"It's a boy!"

Lois and Edwin "Sonny" Johnston welcomed their son on March 28, 1965, at a tiny hospital in Poteau, Oklahoma. The newborn joined eight-year-old sister Elizabeth and six-year-old brother Eddie in the Johnston home. The couple faced pressure to honor their families with the choice of their third child's name. William was Sonny Johnston's dad's name. Theodore was Lois's dad's name. On that spring day the couple introduced William Theodore Johnston to the family. Lois was determined not to have her newborn called Billy, so she immediately referred to the baby as "T." It stuck. William Theodore Johnston would be known as T or W.T. from that point forward.

Sonny Johnston worked for the forest service in Oklahoma. When W.T. was five, Sonny was promoted to district ranger, which meant relocating the family to Virginia, and they moved to the tiny burg of New Castle, Virginia. As a young boy, W.T. suffered from joint pain that the doctor diagnosed as rheumatoid arthritis. He felt stiff and achy each morning, and it was difficult to simply get moving. The doctor recommended what seemed like a rather obvious course of action, something a physician might say when he didn't know what else to prescribe. "Put him in sports and keep him moving." W.T.'s parents pushed their youngest son to get moving, and the activity helped. When Sonny wasn't at work, he and W.T. would play catch and shoot baskets, and he took his son hunting and fishing. Lois signed up W.T. for Little League and tennis.

Sonny had grown up in Hodgen, Oklahoma, just a few miles from the Arkansas state line, bordering the western edge of Ouachita National Forest. He was a bear of a man at six foot three inches tall and 220 pounds. With his size and strength, he likely would have dominated a small-town high school football team, but there was a problem. His high school was so small that basketball was the only sport offered, so that is what he played.

The senior Johnston was a rough and hardworking man with hands so calloused from farm and forest service work that W.T. joked you could strike a match on his dad's palms. Living in rural southeastern Oklahoma, Sonny experienced a sheltered life. The people and culture of the farming community of Hodgen were all he knew. After high school he ventured a couple of hundred miles northwest to Oklahoma State University in Stillwater.

Sonny's limited perception of the world was about to change quickly. The Korean War began, and he left Oklahoma State to enlist in the army. During his basic training, nineteen-year-old Sonny's worldview dramatically expanded. Sonny Johnston had never met, let alone lived with, a black man. He found himself in the Korean War randomly partnered in a life-or-death team relationship with an African American soldier. Sonny later told W.T. that he never had any reservations about his comrade going into battle. Together they faced the enemy and watched out for each other. From their bunker during the bloody conflict, Specialist Green loaded mortars and Sonny fired them. The two soldiers became friends as trust developed in the heat of battle. The men learned that in adversity, it doesn't matter what color a man's skin might be. It only matters if he has your back. That relationship became a harbinger of how the elder Johnston would deal with racial differences in an era when many, if not most, men routinely judged others by color.

When W.T. was seven, the family moved again—halfway across the country from Virginia to Hemphill, Texas. Sonny had been promoted once more and became the district ranger at Sabine National Forest, a lush 160,656-acre piney woods forest that forms part of the boundary between Texas and Louisiana.

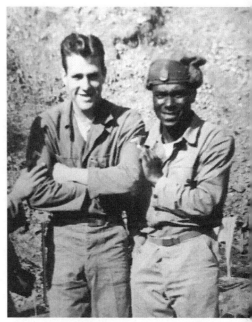

Sonny Johnston and Specialist Green
Courtesy of Elizabeth Henderson

Note – Because of records lost we could not locate Mr. Green's full name. If anyone can help please contact the author at dave@daveburchett.com

Moving to a more diverse community enlarged W.T.'s world just as the military had for his dad. Johnston remembers how anxious he felt on the first day at a new school with no friends. He did not know that he would also interact with African American boys and girls for the first time in his life. Young W.T. had never encountered people who looked different from himself. He remembers feeling intimidated and even a little fearful. His father's response to those emotions would help shape W.T.'s personality forever.

Sonny Johnston shared the story of Specialist Green with his son. He taught him that you treat people the same way you want to be treated, and then he finished with this wise counsel.

"W.T., you judge a man by character and how he treats you. It doesn't matter what he looks like."

Sonny modeled that as a Little League coach in racially charged East Texas. "My dad never treated black kids different. Dad was a rough guy, but also giving and fair with everyone. I got the message from him loud and clear that you ain't born prejudiced. You have to be taught that."

The lesson was driven home by a courageous defense of Curtis Hamilton, the only black youth league coach in the area. He coached W.T.'s Little League team, and the young coach was certainly talented, although perhaps a bit cocky. Hamilton had a simple philosophy. "I didn't care if your daddy was the town drunk or the president of the bank. I played the kids who deserved to play." That strategy didn't sit well with some power brokers who were used to influencing those decisions, and Curtis's color only exacerbated the tension. They wanted him out as coach.

Except for Sonny Johnston. He could not understand why anyone could be so negative about a good man and coach simply because of his skin color. In the midst of the conflict that Coach Hamilton described as catching "holy hell," the attitudes of the men suddenly changed.

Unbeknownst to Hamilton, Sonny Johnston had called a meeting with the other fathers and coaches to discuss the young black coach. He passionately defended Hamilton by presenting facts about the progress Hamilton was making with the development of the boys. Sonny made sure race would not be the issue that would settle this debate. When Sonny Johnston bowed up, you tended to pay attention. "He came ready to reason but prepared to kick some butts," W.T later recalled with a chuckle. The latter proved unnecessary, as Sonny convinced the men to give Curtis Hamilton a chance based on performance.

"He was the only one who would stick out his neck," Hamilton remembers with gratitude. "He changed the whole community by simply standing up for what he thought was the right thing to do. He didn't care what the fallout might be. He just did the right thing because it was the right thing and never told me he had done it. That shows a man's character." In fact, Coach Hamilton was not aware of Sonny Johnston's fiery defense until years later.

Hamilton would go on to coach for the next forty-two years and be a part of two state football championships at Burkeville High School. He still wonders what would have happened if Sonny Johnston had not intervened on his behalf. "It was so discouraging. I felt all alone, and to be honest, I might have given up. I still can't believe it was a white man from Oklahoma who had my back."

One of the foundations of growing up in small-town Texas was church attendance. W.T. found himself at the First United Methodist Church in Hemphill with his mom "every time the doors were open." Lois Johnston was a no-nonsense doer who lived out her faith by serving the least of these. "Mom would find out about kids who needed food or clothes, and she made sure they got what they needed even though we didn't have all that much ourselves." W.T. enjoyed the experience. "At church I lit the candles at the beginning of the service, put them out at the end, and sang in the choir that Mom led."

The Methodist church had one other bonus. It was located next to the Hemphill High School football stadium. Every Monday and Tuesday Lois dutifully showed up for choir practice, and she permitted young W.T. to go watch the Hemphill Hornets practice.

W.T. bounced from school to church to practice, then back to church and home with his mom. He recalls how the years attending the Methodist church are a bittersweet memory. "I was always in church, but my father never went with us." Sonny's absence bothered W.T. immensely; he could not understand why his dad wouldn't join the family for Sunday services. W.T. vowed he would be different if he became a dad someday. But for now, the church offered a spiritual foundation plus a sports connection.

W.T. became a fixture at the Hornets' practices on the days Lois was at church. Hemphill coach Bob Jenkins was an old-school, hard-nosed coach. He noticed the youngster sitting in the bleachers at practice, and one day he gruffly ordered W.T. down to the field. The eight-year-old was taken aback, but it was clear the coach was talking to him. With his mind racing, W.T. nervously made his way to the sideline to face the coach.

"Am I in trouble? Do I have to leave?" W.T. was ready to head back to the church.

Coach Jenkins sized the boy up and asked gruffly, "What's your name, Son?"

"They call me W.T., sir."

"Well, W.T., we need your help."

At Hornet Stadium, the building housing the public bathrooms was located at the edge of the end zone, creating an ongoing dilemma. When the kicker practiced extra points and field goals, the footballs would often end up stranded on the bathroom roof. That evening, practice had ground to a halt because they were out of footballs. Coach Jenkins walked the fourth grader over to the building and boosted him onto the roof.

"I need you to toss those footballs down to us so we can keep practicing."

W.T. quickly retrieved the balls, and practice continued; the job began W.T.'s relationship with football, which would last the rest of his life. Perhaps W.T.'s persistence impressed the coach, or maybe he saw a bit of himself in the youngster's tenacity. By the time the season began, W.T. was given a job as a team manager and even allowed to travel on the team bus.

For the next two years, W.T. was on the Hemphill sideline, experiencing the sounds, emotions, exhilaration, and heartbreak of competition. There was little doubt in his mind what his career path would be. Someday he would coach. At least that would be his fallback plan if his dream to be the Dallas Cowboys' quarterback somehow didn't work out.

One of W.T.'s key duties was getting the halftime refreshments ready for the team.

"About two minutes before the half ended, Coach Jenkins would give me the nod. I would race to the locker room and pull out wooden cases of warm Coca-Cola and grab a bottle opener. I needed to have thirty-six twelve-ounce glass bottles ready when the team came in. One night I decided to take a swig out of each bottle—more than three dozen Cokes. I did it so fast that I got sicker than a dog, and I was throwing up on the sideline as the second half started."

"What's wrong with you?" Coach Jenkins asked.

W.T. confessed what he had done, and Coach sent him home. The incident was never mentioned again. That was another early lesson for W.T. When you suffer consequences from your bad decisions, that may be all you need. W.T. didn't need a lecture to bring the lesson home; he had learned the hard way.

During the 1974 football season, the second-year team manager had an up-close look at the Newton High School team from the Hemphill sideline, and he was awestruck by how good they were. They played with speed and skills that were different from the rest of the teams he had seen. W.T. was not surprised at all when Newton clinched the state championship that year.

As he grew older, W.T.'s passions were hunting, fishing, and sports. He played every sport, but he especially loved the passion and teamwork of football. By junior high he was a rawboned and tough athlete for Hemphill Junior High. Coach Jenkins had watched the young boy absorb the techniques and nuances at practice as a team manager. Now that he was growing big and strong, Jenkins had to be excited about the prospect of having this young man in a Hornet's uniform in a few years.

During a seventh-grade football game in Hemphill, W.T. demonstrated that he had learned from his dad's example. Maybe his father had not been the spiritual leader that W.T. had desired, but his practical lessons about how to treat others had made a difference. Perhaps it is impossible to be truly color-blind, yet W.T. had learned from his dad that you can be color indifferent and, more importantly, color courageous. It seems outrageous today, but it was not unheard of in the '70s for white and black athletes to drink from different water bottles. The team was integrated, but the message was obvious: The players were not equal. Their water bottles were segregated, clearly labeled.

"I remember grabbing one of the black kids' water bottles, putting my lips on the spout, and drinking deeply. Some of the white kids looked at me in horror," Johnston recalls with a smile.

"What are you doing?" a white teammate blurted.

W.T.'s answer was simple.

"I'm thirsty."

W.T. Johnston never looked for the easy or politically correct response. He learned to look for truth that would quench his thirst in every aspect of his life. That would become his lifelong quest.

2

MAMA TRIED

That inner quest for truth was noble, but it would prove to be a difficult journey. Change was about to disrupt W.T.'s idyllic childhood in Hemphill.

In the winter of 1978, Sonny moved his family to Hot Springs, Arkansas, located on the eastern side of the Ouachita Mountains he had loved as a boy in Oklahoma. Moving from small-town Hemphill, where practically everyone knew everyone and their business, to the vacation destination of Hot Springs was a monumental change. For W.T., it was going from a rural setting to a big city—from a small school whose entire student body totaled only a few more students than the graduating class of four hundred at Hot Springs.

Not only were there more kids, but drugs were easily available and in shocking quantities at his new high school. The privileged white kids preferred cocaine, but marijuana was cheaper.

W.T. fell in with an older crowd and started going with them to bars when he was fifteen. "I just fit in best with the hell-raising crowd," W.T. recalls. Unbeknownst to Sonny and Lois, W.T. and his buddies would skip school and sneak into Oaklawn Park Race Track. Although the friends he was hanging around with were regular drug users and pot smokers, W.T. never joined in. He did drink, though. A lot. Sonny and Lois were also unaware that their son was heading down that path.

W.T. and his best friend, Mike Tankersly, remember that they often "acted like knuckleheads." Fortunately for them, there was no social media or phone cameras to document their behavior. They scuffled with others a lot, but no one dreamed of bringing a weapon to a fight. They just fought it out with their fists, and then it was over. Sonny knew W.T. was fighting now and then, but Lois was blissfully unaware.

W.T. Johnston and Mike Tankersly on the infamous Dodge Pickup
(Courtesy Debbie Johnston)

The biggest problem for the football players was when someone went too far and the coaches found out. They had a painful way to take care of the indiscretions, and they delighted in making miscreants run "gassers." These were all-out sprints from one sideline to the other, repeated four times, and then run again and again. All you need to know is that the players called it the "puke drill." This was also an era when the paddle was still an option and one that was utilized freely. Bonding moments like that with the coaches kept athletes a bit more well behaved, or at least stealthier in their activities.

Mike spent a lot of time at W.T.'s house, which became a refuge for him. His parents didn't set boundaries for their teenage son. Mike was left to fend for himself—until he met W.T. and his family. It didn't take long for Lois to become a second mother to Mike, and she gave him a much-needed sense of normalcy.

Of course, the two friends were not always supervised.

One night, they started throwing darts at each other in W.T.'s room, not thinking of the myriad things that could go horribly wrong. The dartboard was long gone, but the sharp steel-tipped weapons were still around. The weapons were zinged across the room, the two opponents dodging, laughing, grabbing, laughing, retaliating, and laughing even harder. And then they both saw it—the perfect target mounted on the wall.

Neither one of them knows for sure who nailed the deciding shot that ended the game. Mike was just thankful that he and W.T. still had both of their eyes when W.T. called it a night and Mike left.

The next morning Sonny walked into his son's bedroom and did a double take. Was he seeing correctly? Were those hundreds of tiny punctures in the wall? As he scanned the room, he froze. Was he imagining what he saw? No, a prized trophy bass *was* impaled, the "spear" embedded in the gills. W.T. had caught the fish as a young boy, and Sonny had paid hard-earned money to have the fish mounted.

The elder Johnston was not amused. He was livid. Even a chiseled athlete like W.T. shrank from Sonny when he was riled up.

A few minutes later, Mike got a phone call from his dart-tossing opponent.

"You need to get over here right away!" W.T. said. "My dad has flipped his gourd."

Sonny met Mike at the door. The chastised boys issued a quiet "Yes, sir" to Sonny's demand that the walls be repaired before he got home. The two culprits spent the rest of the morning filling those hundred-plus dart holes with spackle, followed by a fresh paint job. The bass couldn't be spackled, so from that point on, the fish had an extra pinhole in its anatomy.

Not surprisingly, when the Johnstons moved to Hot Springs, Lois immediately found a church home at the Piney Grove Methodist Church. She insisted that W.T. attend regularly, although her rebellious teenager did his best not to. Lois might have been naive about W.T.'s Saturday night activities, but she was unrelenting on what his Sunday morning schedule would be. W.T. tried to share his misery by dragging his buddy Mike along. In hindsight, Mike realizes it was a lifesaver for both of them.

"I think the truth we absorbed there made a difference. The teaching W.T. reluctantly received kept him centered and helped keep me centered. I was much wilder than W.T. My parents didn't care what I did. But Lois cared, and I felt like I couldn't let her down. I shudder to think what my life would have looked like if God had not dropped the Johnston family into my world."

In some ways W.T. emulated the rebellious wayward son in Merle Haggard's haunting song "Mama Tried." He walked a perilous line of raising hell—sticking one foot over—but unlike in Haggard's song, W.T. always pulled it back before it ruined his future. He knew if he got in trouble, his sports eligibility could be affected. Thinking back, he also believes his mother's influence and prayers kept him from doing something he would regret for the rest of his life.

Still, W.T. spent weekends cruising up and down Main Street in Hot Springs, looking for good times but more often finding trouble. "We drank, partied, and fought. That is what we did."

One night, things went terribly south. "Some guys had jumped my friends, and Mike picked me up to go and confront them. We found out that the guys were in the high school parking lot, so I devised this brilliant plan to get them. I would pull my red 1978 Dodge Ram pickup right up against the passenger door of their car, so they could only get out on one side. Then my buddies would pile out of the bed of the pickup and punch them as they piled out."

W.T.'s plan was foiled in a hurry when one of the punks pulled out a gun and pointed it at his temple.

"Do you want me to get out now?" the thug taunted.

In a split second, W.T. threw the truck in reverse and, with screeching tires, hauled out of there amidst a flurry of bullets. The punks followed W.T. and his friends to the Johnstons' house. When Sonny heard the commotion and ran outside, the pursuers quickly retreated.

Today, W.T. shakes his head at how differently that night could have turned out. "My story could have ended right there—another young fool who wasted his God-given potential."

For all his reckless behavior, W.T. got one thing right: Debra Short. The two of them met when W.T. started attending Lake Hamilton. Debbie was a beautiful brunette who was immediately attracted to Johnston. But there was a problem. Debbie was two grades ahead of him, and that was a social no-no in 1979. After a few months they shook off the social mores and began dating in Debbie's senior and W.T.'s sophomore year.

Ironically, they became close after a football coach asked Debbie to tutor W.T. She saw something special in this talented but hot-tempered kid. She fell in love with him even though not everyone approved of her committing to someone who had a reputation as a hell-raising partyer. Debbie's parents never saw that side of Johnston because he was wisely quiet and very mannerly around the Short family.

Debbie had been raised in a strict religious home, but she had also strayed a bit from her upbringing. "I had put my faith on the back burner. Like W.T., I went to church every Sunday, but I was not living like I should. Still, I felt the conviction of what I knew was right, and I am sure that kept me from straying too far."

Besides Debbie, the one thing that kept Johnston grounded was sports. Football was king in Arkansas, and W.T. was a gifted quarterback for the Lake Hamilton Wolves. Mike bragged about his best friend's talent. "He had a cannon of an arm. In fact, the receivers had a hard time holding on to the lasers that W.T. fired at them. He probably would have been a big-time prospect, but he suffered a couple of knee injuries, and they couldn't repair them like they can today."

Lake Hamilton QB W.T. Johnston
(Courtesy Debbie Johnston)

Some folks convinced Sonny Johnston that W.T. would have a better shot at garnering a college scholarship playing for a bigger high school. They talked to Hot Springs coach Joe Reese about transferring W.T. for his senior year. The Johnstons moved to another district, and W.T. started his final year of football at Hot Springs High School in the fall of 1982.

Coach Reese was old school and a deadly serious coach who had played one season for the Green Bay Packers and Vince Lombardi. For W.T., the transition from a small school to the biggest school in town was tougher than he had expected. "I played, but I was never accepted. Not fitting in led me on a search for relevancy that would last for a few frustrating years. Looking back, I can see that my path was like a country song. I was lookin' for meaning in all the wrong places."

His senior year was a roller coaster of winning ups and losing downs. "I remember playing Little Rock Parkview. They were one of the best teams in Arkansas, and they had one of the best players in the country." Keith Jackson was a *Parade* all-American at tight end and safety. He would go on to an all-American career at Oklahoma and become a six-time Pro Bowler with the Green Bay Packers, including a Super Bowl win.

On that night the upstart Hot Springs Trojans shut out the highly favored Parkview Patriots, and W.T. received the game ball for his play. The season with the Trojans went well enough that it caught the attention of Kevin Gundy, the recruiting coordinator of Fort Scott Community College in Fort Scott, Kansas. He offered W.T. a scholarship when he graduated from Hot Springs. If W.T. performed well at the school in Kansas, it would likely lead to an opportunity to play Division I college football.

Of course, W.T. had a memorable going-away party that started with a fight. It was a night Mike can't forget. "W.T. and I were pretty big guys, so I guess they had prepared themselves. We started to mix it up, and these guys pulled out a canister and maced us!"

Talk about breaking an unwritten rule for real-men confrontations! W.T. did not take it well. He got his licks in but also suffered a broken nose in the farewell melee.

In the car on the way home, W.T. kept babying his hand.

"Is there something wrong with your hand?" Mike looked at W.T.

"Naw, it's just throbbing. I'm sure it will stop when I ice it."

They stopped for ice, but it didn't help much.

W.T. couldn't hide his injury from his parents, but he initially didn't reveal to them how bad it actually was. He decided he had disappointed them enough during his high school years.

But after days of agony, W.T. went to a doctor. He had broken several bones in his passing hand, and the doctor casted him up to his elbow.

"How long do I have to wear the cast?" W.T. asked.

"At least six weeks. Maybe longer."

W.T. had a slight problem. Training camp for the Fort Scott Greyhounds started in three.

W.T. loaded up his red pickup and headed more than three hundred miles north to Kansas. The broken hand was a temporary nuisance that he decided not to mention to Coach Gary Butler. He managed to keep things under wraps when he arrived, but the day before camp started, the cast had to go. W.T. bought some tin snips, cut off the cast, and showed up at practice as if nothing had happened. It quickly became apparent that something was amiss.

"It hurt really bad taking snaps from center and handing the ball off. Plus I could barely grip the ball to throw it."

Fort Scott's hot prospect was struggling, a far cry from the strong-armed quarterback Gundy had recruited. Finally, he sat Johnston down.

"What's going on with you, W.T.? You can barely hold the ball."

"I broke my hand a couple of weeks ago ..."

Another trip to the doctor and X-rays confirmed the story—the bones that had been healing were splintered again. Once again, W.T.'s hand was immobilized with a cast. His first year of playing football was over, and his scholarship was pulled.

W.T. didn't take the news well. He wanted to punch something, but look what had happened already. He just wanted to play football—somewhere. But not at Fort Scott. Again he had disappointed Sonny and his long-suffering mom. They were upset he had lost his scholarship but okay with W.T. transferring and getting a second chance.

Coach Butler graciously set up an interview for the restless athlete to meet with legendary coach Lou Holtz at Arkansas. Johnston headed to Fayetteville for the meeting. En route, he stopped for gas, and while standing at the pump, he began thinking.

Coach Holtz doesn't know me from Adam's house cat. This will be a waste of my time.

So W.T. paid for the gas, decided to ditch the interview, and drove past the Razorback campus.

Thankfully, someone he knew lived in Fayetteville. W.T. and Mike Tankersly had stayed in touch after their high school exploits.

"Mike, it's W.T. I'm here in Fayetteville and was wondering if I could crash at your place."

W.T. had a place to stay, but no place to play. He was getting antsy.

Again, a kind coach offered to help. Coach Kevin Gundy called Larry Lacewell, head coach of the Arkansas State University Red Wolves, and asked if he would give Johnston a look. (The coach knew talent when he saw it. In 1992, Lacewell became the director of scouting for the Dallas Cowboys.) Coach Lacewell agreed to give W.T. a chance as a walk-on.

He redshirted and attempted to let his hand heal. His obstinate refusal to let the injury heal properly would have a lasting effect, as W.T. admits. "To this day, it hurts to shake hands."

W.T. finally had football to look forward to, but he quickly slipped into his undisciplined ways. Partying was more fun than going to class. After all, isn't that what college is about? The lure of Beale Street in Memphis was a fairly easy drive from Fayetteville, and it took a toll on W.T.'s academics. He ended up with a 1.3 GPA for the first semester. And as for football? He was getting the crap beaten out of him on the scout team.

Most young athletes' stories end when they become underachieving nomads. But something continued to drive W.T. He knew he wasn't living right. As much as he didn't want to disappoint his parents, he knew he already had. He knew being held "hostage" in church all those years with his mom had planted something better in his heart. And yet ...

"I wasn't ready to act on it. I wanted to be in control."

W.T. missed Debbie; she had always helped calm him down. She was in Hot Springs, attending classes at Garland County Community College. They had stayed in touch, but Debbie was beginning to wonder if he would ever be settled. W.T. needed to figure things out quickly or he could lose not only his football dream but also the love of his life.

3

DIARY OF A FOOTBALL NOMAD

W.T. had hoped to be piling up passing yardage on the gridiron; instead, he was piling up mileage on his red pickup. He refused to give up his football dream. After a year at Arkansas State, the coaches saw the passion that Johnston had for football. They knew he could play, but he needed to transfer a bit of that passion to the classroom. The coaches gave him another lifeline: "If you go to a junior college and get your grades in order, you will be welcome back here." Next stop? Northwest Mississippi Community College in Senatobia, Mississippi. W.T. hoped he could get his grades and football priorities aligned there.

Johnston played spring ball for the Rangers, but before the season began, he got a call from someone who had never forgotten his talent.

Former Fort Scott recruiter Kevin Gundy had joined the coaching staff at Peru State College in Peru, Nebraska. When head coach Jay Adcox said he was looking for a quarterback, Gundy remembered W.T. *It's been more than a year. His hand should have healed by now.* The coaching world is a small universe, and it did not take long for Gundy to track the wandering athlete down. The Ranger coach gave Gundy the dormitory phone number, and to his surprise, W.T. heard his former coach describing a new chance to play at Peru State. It didn't really matter to Johnston if he had heard of Peru State or even knew where it was located. He knew what his answer would be if the offer officially came.

"How about it, W.T.? Want to play for the Bobcats?"

W.T. did what he did best at this point in his life. He packed up the pickup and headed to the Cornhusker State.

Over eighteen months, W.T. had worn four different jerseys in four different states: Greyhounds (Kansas), Red Wolves (Arkansas), Rangers (Mississippi), and now Bobcats (Nebraska). He knew he had screwed up every opportunity that coaches had given him, but he hoped for another chance. Peru, Nebraska, turned out to be a good fit. W.T. settled down and concentrated on playing the game he loved.

Coach Gundy saw W.T.'s best qualities emerge. The impressive athlete was shaping up as a vocal and encouraging leader, always trying to lift up his teammates. He was a true team player; it was never about him.

It had been a long time since W.T. had been in one place long enough to completely unpack. Now he figured he would see if someone else would do some packing.

On Christmas Eve in 1984, W.T. was back home in Hot Springs. That night he had slipped a small box into his jacket pocket. He and Debbie had discussed marriage, but it seemed impractical with W.T. in Nebraska and Debbie still in Hot Springs.

In typical W.T. fashion, he determined the details could be figured out later. He wanted to be with Debra Short for the rest of his life.

The proposal may have lacked romance, but then, W.T. was never much of a romantic.

"Reach in my pocket," W.T. directed Debbie.

"Why?"

"I have something there for you."

Debbie slipped her hand in W.T.'s pocket and felt a small box. She knew what the "something" was.

"So?" the always erudite W.T. queried.

"Yes!" Debbie replied and hugged her future husband.

She was happy that she wouldn't be away from W.T. anymore. But at the same time, it was scary to leave her family for the first time.

They were married in Hot Springs on August 3, 1985, and squeezed in a

W.T. and Debbie share a laugh.
(Courtesy Debbie Johnston)

whirlwind honeymoon to Gulf Shores, Alabama, and Biloxi, Mississippi. The honeymoon was cut short in what would prove to be a harbinger of Debbie Johnston's life ahead. Football camp was starting, and W.T. had to be back. The couple moved into campus housing in Peru, and W.T. got back on the field. His college football dream was finally a reality, at least for the next two seasons in Nebraska. Johnston was a solid contributor and exceptional leader at quarterback for the Bobcats.

At the end of the 1986 season, Coach Adcox and Coach Gundy were relieved of their duties. W.T. was getting a foretaste of how difficult and transient a coach's life could be. Coach Gundy returned to Fort Scott. W.T. was grateful to the man who had given him that last and best chance to follow his dream. One of W.T.'s strongest traits surfaced again. Loyalty.

Perhaps the next coaching staff would find a place for him, but who knew? Plus, it would be hard to play for another coach with the indebtedness he felt to Coach Gundy. But there was another problem.

He couldn't follow Coach Gundy back to a junior college. He had to find a four-year school to finish out. With Debbie beside him, he loaded up the pickup and took off searching for another place that fit.

This time his old high school coach Joe Reese came to the rescue and put W.T. in touch with legendary coach Sporty Carpenter at Henderson State in Arkadelphia, Arkansas. Carpenter agreed to give W.T. a shot, and the athlete added "Reddies" to his collection of team nicknames and football jerseys. At Henderson he became fast friends with offensive lineman Jack Alvarez. Jack knew from his days as a high school standout at DeSoto Academy that W.T. had been one of the top high school quarterbacks in Arkansas, but snaps were hard to come by for a newcomer at Henderson. W.T. was buried on the depth chart and longed to get on the field.

A week into the season, W.T. was moved to tight end. Jack Alvarez remembers that offensive coordinator Bill Massey was merciless on the senior transfer as the coaches tested his mettle. W.T. never complained. His attitude hadn't changed from when he was at Peru—he just wanted to contribute to the team and help them win, no matter what position he played. His fellow teammates respected him for that selfless spirit. The coaching staff also saw his team-first competitiveness and shifted him to outside linebacker. It was a perfect fit.

Jack and the other players were regular dinner guests at W.T. and Debbie's apartment. Debbie somehow managed to prepare a feast of tacos or spaghetti for ravenous jocks on a shoestring budget. The couple's ongoing hospitality was another way they put others before themselves. The players always joked that Debbie was way tougher than W.T., not taking any crap from them!

Debbie enjoyed making their little apartment the gathering spot for W.T.'s teammates. It helped her be part of her husband's community.

W.T. had achieved his lifelong goal of playing college football. The Dallas Cowboys quarterback dream? It was looking more and more unlikely, but overall his life was good. The Reddie was part of a football community, sharing hard knocks and life with men who had his back. He was married to a smart and beautiful woman. After multiple false starts and hasty departures from school, he was set to graduate with a bachelor of science in education. He knew he wanted to continue his football life by coaching after graduation. Life was finally beginning to make sense.

And added to that was the unexpected news that Debbie was pregnant with their first child.

———————◆———————

The baby was due to be born soon after the football season of W.T.'s senior year. Perhaps because the baby shared W.T.'s DNA, the about-to-be-newborn decided to do the unexpected and change things up. Johnston came home exhausted from a tough practice and vaguely heard these words from Debbie as he stumbled into the bedroom to rest:

"My water broke a little while ago."

As if in a scene from a TV sitcom, Johnston was too tired to process that information until he got into the bedroom and replayed it in his brain. To be fair to W.T., the baby was not due for two months, and Debbie's going into labor was not yet on his radar. Finally, it sank in that this baby was on the way, and he raced into action as only W.T. Johnston could.

W.T. was still wearing his athletic shorts, but there was only time to grab some shoes and get Debbie into the car. Since he didn't know how long they would be gone, he threw the dog in the back of the truck too.

The hospital was in Hot Springs, and W.T. began a frantic rush to cover the thirty-five miles between Arkadelphia and Hot Springs in record time.

"I was going eighty-five miles per hour, and suddenly I see flashing lights behind me. An Arkansas state trooper pulled me over, and I needed to let him know that we did not have time for this."

Imagine the surprise of this trooper when a chiseled 230-pound man in shorts and a T-shirt started running toward the squad car with a panicked and wild-eyed look.

"He drew his gun and started yelling at me to get my ass back in the car," W.T. recalls with a chuckle. W.T. didn't know that an Arkansas state trooper had been killed two weeks earlier while pulling over a vehicle. A less restrained officer or perhaps W.T.'s taking another step or two forward could have resulted in a truly tragic mishap. When W.T. relocated his posterior as directed, he was able to explain his driving speed and his poorly thought out approach to the trooper. Once again God was protecting his child.

"It went from adversarial confrontation to that trooper becoming our guardian angel, as he gave us a high-speed, legal escort to the emergency room."

When they arrived, the doctors rushed Debbie into the delivery room, while other medical staff pulled W.T. aside to explain all the possible outcomes of the baby's early arrival. The baby would likely be dangerously underweight. If the newborn weighed less than five pounds, the child would have to be airlifted to Little Rock, where neonatal intensive care could be provided. Johnston read the papers that stated he understood the baby could die on that journey. If the child survived, there could be developmental issues. There was a real concern that the baby's lungs would not be developed enough for the newborn to breathe unaided. All of this was overwhelming to the father-to-be as he signed the papers to authorize the emergency transfer to Little Rock if necessary, with an outcome he could not control.

But the situation was in Someone's control. That was something W.T.'s mother had always taught him. He could hear her voice, almost as if she were sitting next to him in the waiting room. "When you don't know where to turn, you turn to God." He knew what he needed to do.

"I went to the chapel in the hospital, and for the first time in my life, I got on my knees and prayed in earnest. I begged for my baby's life."

While he waited, W.T. found a pay phone and let Lois and Sonny know their newest grandchild was on the way sooner than expected. The excited and anxious grandparents drove through the night from Oklahoma to Hot Springs. Lois added her prayers to the petitions her son offered in the chapel.

God answered their prayers. William Andrew (Drew) Johnston surprised the doctors by checking in at more than five pounds. The newborn's lungs were developed enough for him to breathe on his own after a few days with supplemental oxygen. Drew would have to wait for his first helicopter ride. Despite the doctor's concerns, W.T. and Debbie's firstborn suffered no developmental issues, although today W.T. is not sure that is completely accurate.

"Drew is very directionally challenged, so I sometimes wonder," W.T. says with a big smile.

W.T. and Debbie both believed that the prayers for their son had been answered—Drew was healthy. For all the years W.T. had gone to church with Lois, he had never been as honest with God as he was in that hospital chapel.

"I needed God's help, and He met me there. But when everything turned out okay, I went back to my own self-interests."

4

ON THE MOVE AGAIN ... AND AGAIN

Drew's surprise entrance changed a lot of things. W.T. and Debbie did not return to their place in Arkadelphia. Sonny and W.T. packed their meager belongings, and they temporarily moved in with Debbie's mom, Alice, and stepdad, Coy Burroughs. It was a bit surreal for Debbie to be back in the home where she had spent her high school years. But the young couple appreciated the free lodging after Drew was released from the hospital and the family prepared for the next season of their life. That transition included renting a house in Little Rock. W.T. had already been assigned his student teaching gig in Little Rock beginning in the new year.

"Our life was chaos," Debbie remembers. "We had hoped to finish college before having kids, but God had other ideas. I was a nervous wreck and, as usual, W.T. was calm." And Drew? Debbie's parents spoiled their newest grandchild with tons of attention.

After graduation, W.T. had hoped to be a college graduate assistant, but the financial needs of a newborn and wife forced him to turn down

BETWEEN THE WHITE LINES

opportunities at Northeast Louisiana (now Louisiana Monroe) and Henderson State.

Johnston landed his first opportunity to coach at Linden-Kildare High School in East Texas. Linden is noted as Music City, Texas, claiming famous ragtime pianist Scott Joplin and legendary blues guitar player and singer T-Bone Walker as native sons. Another resident of Linden tried out for the Tiger football team in the early 1960s, but his coach feared he was too small and suggested he join the marching band instead. The young man took to music quite well, and he started his own band. Don Henley would eventually sell 150 million albums—and counting—as the drummer and colead vocalist of the Eagles.

The football program at Linden-Kildare High School was not quite as renowned as those music superstars. Rodney Russell was the new head coach, and he brought Johnston on board to coach quarterbacks and defensive ends for the Tigers. Like most small-town coaches, Johnston wore multiple hats. He also coached basketball and baseball and taught driver's education.

More than a year later, Drew gave the young couple another health scare. The fifteen-month-old toddler had been taking antibiotics for a couple of weeks to treat a stubborn fever and flu-like symptoms. The medicine did not seem to be helping. When Drew became lethargic and the skin around his eyes became dark like a raccoon's, Debbie and W.T. knew something was terribly wrong.

East Texas was experiencing an ice storm, and Texans know that weather events like that shut down everything. But W.T. and Debbie felt they could not risk waiting, and they set out for the best hospital in the area—sixty miles away in Texarkana. W.T. again found himself asking God for help as the red truck with its precious cargo slipped and slid to the hospital. Somehow the family got there safely.

Drew was very ill, and the couple could only hope that they had gotten to the hospital in time to help him. The first fear was that Drew had meningitis, and W.T. still recalls the heartbreak of holding his son as doctors did a spinal tap on his tiny back. "He was scared with all of the lights and commotion. His cry broke my heart, and I remember his eyes looking at me to protect him, and I couldn't. It is so hard to watch your child go through pain and fear, but we had to find out what was going on to get him better. I couldn't keep him from the pain, but I could be there for him." The lab results were positive for bacterial meningitis, but the antibiotics Drew had been taking likely kept a full-blown case from developing. The doctors treated him for the potentially deadly disease as the young parents anxiously marked each passing hour as a good sign.

Debbie believed in the power of prayer, and the Christian community responded. Their local church set up an around-the-clock prayer chain with folks asking God to heal baby Drew. A great-aunt brought a prayer cloth and pinned it on Drew's pillow. God met the family again, and Drew recovered after four days in the hospital. Like the Israelites of the Old Testament, W.T. and Debbie were grateful for God's mercy. And like the Israelites, they got on with their life after Drew was healthy and put God back on the sideline.

———◆———

Coaching Texas high school football is an extremely competitive career, and young football coaches must chase opportunities no matter how inconvenient they might be. At this point in the process, the one thing the Johnstons knew as well as football was how to move. After a year at Linden, Johnston had a chance to join respected coach Brownie Parmley. Parmley had enjoyed a storied career at Bolton High School in Alexandria, Louisiana. He had originally called Jack Alvarez to see if he would join his staff. Alvarez was content with his role as a graduate assistant at McNeese State, but he recommended his friend for the position. Parmley brought Johnston in to coach the defense in 1990.

At Bolton, coaches and players began to see how W.T. Johnston could be a difference maker between the white lines. The Bolton Bears had some offensive talent, but the defense looked suspect at best in spring practice. By the time the season started, the defense was more than holding its own. Star lineman Mike McDaniel was interviewed by the Alexandria newspaper, the *Town Talk*, and asked why the defense had shown such significant improvement in a short period of time.

"Coach Johnston got on us," recalled McDaniel. "We got tired of that, tired of getting yelled at."

W.T. would prefer that be understood as "coaching up" a group of kids, but either way, it showed an ability to reach kids, challenge them, and make a difference on the field.

While W.T. was coaching at Bolton, he and Debbie welcomed Joshua Shaw to the family in February of 1991. In keeping with the family tradition, Shaw decided to make his appearance while W.T. was in the middle of a sports season. W.T. was coaching baseball for the Bolton Bears when Debbie went into labor.

Bolton provided W.T. with solid coaching experience, and he loved working for Parmley, but there was an itch to get back to Texas. His former brother-in-law Robbie Walker had worked in Newton, Texas, for legendary coach Curtis Barbay. When a job opened, Walker suggested that Barbay might want to interview Johnston. There was an immediate bond between Coach Barbay and W.T. The four Johnstons were on their way to Newton, Texas, to become part of the Newton High School family.

5

THE TOWN THAT TIME FORGOT

Newton, Texas, was a far cry from Hot Springs, Arkansas.

To W.T. and Debbie, it was like moving to Mayberry, USA—minus Sheriff Andy Taylor and Deputy Barney Fife. In many ways, it was a town that time passed by, definitely not as "progressive" as many of the places where the Johnstons had lived. And yet, the young family began to see the real advantages of living in a small town where people knew each other and had one another's backs. W.T. and Debbie began to see this move as a blessing.

It was impossible to know at the time how much of an added blessing it would be for W.T. to work with Coach Curtis Barbay, one of the most renowned coaches in Texas prep football.

Barbay was a genius of the game, and W.T. was an eager student. He was in awe of what the Newton head coach did with his team. "Coach Barbay could see things on the football field that other coaches couldn't. He knew exactly where the other team was going to go when they lined up, and no one could match his moves. Coach could move his checkers on the board better than any coach I have ever seen."

Newton ran an offense that was installed by Coach Lidney Thompson in 1968. Thompson first saw it as a junior high coach with Port Neches-Groves. He diagrammed an interesting formation while scouting upcoming opponent Nederland. He called it the "Scat Play," and Thompson installed that offense when he became the Itasca Wampus Cats head coach in 1967. It fit the skills of tough, quick players who were willing to do the dirty work of blocking, and it only required a quick back to succeed. From that seemingly simple set-and-read formation, there were literally hundreds of variables to befuddle opponents.

Another key moment in the history of Newton football had happened the summer of 1968. Coach Thompson was playing a round of golf at Pleasure Island in Port Arthur. The conversation turned to assistant coaches, and Thompson casually mentioned he needed to hire an assistant. His golf partner that day knew of a young man playing in another foursome who was seeking a job. And that is how Curtis Barbay became an Eagle. He and his wife, Mona, decided to give Newton a one-year trial because it was closer to the lakes he loved to fish.

Those years were not exactly glamorous for the coaching staff. Weights were fashioned from iron pipes attached to cement filled paint cans. The school lacked laundry facilities, so every Saturday morning, the coaches assembled at the local laundromat to wash the uniforms from the night before. Principal John Singletary would collect quarters from the school vending machines to feed the washers and dryers. While the socks, shirts, and jockstraps spun around, the coaches would spread out game plans on the laundry folding tables and plot the strategy for the next game.

Lidney Thompson was an innovator as well. The coaches would evaluate every single play of the previous game and hand out a grade sheet to each player. The specific assignment and results of every play by all eleven on the field were carefully graded. Then the team watched the game film with their grade sheets in hand. It was a remarkable teaching tool to both correct and affirm players. It was a great motivator to play hard and smart on every play because the grades were coming and the film would be reviewed on Monday.

Lidney Thompson after his first playoff win in 1972.
(Courtesy Bobby Bean)

The coaches began teaching their offense and defense at all levels, so the players knew the Newton way well before they got to high school.

Coach Thompson changed the culture and set the expectation bar that would become Purple Pride. When he was first introduced in the high school teachers' lounge, he was sarcastically welcomed to the "graveyard of coaches." Thompson changed that reputation for good.

———◆———

Each year, the program grew stronger, and by 1974 the Newton Eagles had reached the pinnacle with their first state title. After that season, Lidney Thompson turned the reins over to Curtis Barbay. And now Coach Barbay was teaching W.T. the simple offense that was maddeningly complex for opposing defenses. "We lined up in a very simple set, but we had thousands of formations within that set. Coach Barbay could always exploit the other team's defense with a matchup formation they couldn't stop." Barbay taught his new staff member the keys to seeing those mismatches, and W.T. was a quick study. But there were bigger lessons that the coaching mentor passed along, life lessons that he knew W.T. needed to learn.

Even though W.T. had matured a lot since marrying Debbie and becoming a father, he was still a hothead on the field when a kid didn't put in the work. When that happened, he was ready to bench that player or even run him off. W.T. expressed his frustration in no uncertain terms to Coach Barbay.

Barbay listened, then said, "It's not our job to run kids off. It is our job to fix them and grow them into men."

As important as the game was to Coach Barbay, the young athletes were significantly more important. He had a huge heart for kids. Yes, teaching them football skills and how to work as a team was gratifying, but instilling self-worth in them was the primary goal. That was a value they would carry for the rest of their lives. Both men knew that many of the boys came from homes where they didn't receive any validation.

W.T. had seen the head coach's philosophy in action, but it didn't sink in until Coach Barbay sat him down and said it. "So many times, I have more confidence in these young men than they have in themselves. I have to convince them of their value as athletes and men."

Part of that wisdom was not to run up the score on other teams. Sometimes W.T. struggled with that idea. "I often looked at the coach on the other sideline and wanted to run it up on them. Coach Barbay never did that to the kids. He knew the opposing team's coach would eventually forget that rout or have his chance for payback. But the kids don't forget those humiliations."

During the 1992 and 1993 Newton football seasons, W.T. grew close to Curtis Barbay—the only man who was closer to W.T. was Sonny. Barbay was tough and old school, but he also possessed a wicked sense of humor. He was known to enjoy the racetrack in nearby Shreveport, Louisiana. Former player Tommy Stivender remembers walking to the practice field when Barbay fell in beside him and shared how he had taken all the toilets out of his house. Stivender took the bait. "What happened, Coach?"

Barbay got a twinkle in his eye and replied, "I lost my rear end at the track, and I don't need them anymore."

Barbay taught his protégé W.T. Johnston how to win on and off the field. But the siren song of career advancement tempted Johnston once again. Rodney Russell, the head coach from Linden, was now at the helm of Little Cypress-Mauriceville High School near Beaumont, Texas. He offered the twenty-eight-year-old coach a chance to be the offensive coordinator for a Texas 4A program. To jump from being a 3A position coach to being a 4A coordinator was almost unheard of, so the decision was obvious. W.T. and Debbie started packing.

The Johnstons packed up the house they had rented in Newton and settled in Orange, Texas, some twenty-five miles from Beaumont. The suburban community was wealthy and predominately white. The team showed real promise under Coach Russell, but something was missing for W.T. The fans were happy with a winning record. W.T. had grown used to the sky-high aspirations of the Newton Eagles fans. If you didn't go deep in the play-offs, it was a down year.

Growing up in Hemphill, getting his first coaching job at Linden, and spending two years with Coach Barbay in Newton, W.T. had become attached to the hardscrabble kids who played their hearts out for those teams. That's the kind of program he loved the most. He wanted to go back to Newton.

He called Coach Barbay and told him his heart was purple through and through. Barbay was pleased to hear from W.T., but the only spot he had open was offensive line coach—a step backward from W.T.'s coordinator position in Orange. But that didn't matter. W.T. longed to return to the Eagles—he knew there was plenty more to learn from his mentor. So in 1994, the Johnstons left the Gulf and headed north.

They contacted the owners of the house they had rented and made an offer to buy it. The deal was accepted, but the family now renting the house refused to vacate. What now? W.T.'s college buddy Jack Alvarez invited the Johnston family to live with his family in nearby Jasper, but everyone knew this wasn't a long-term solution. Jack and his wife, Kim, had two rambunctious boys of their own, which meant—all total—eight people were sharing a three-bedroom home.

Back in Newton, the obstinate family refused to budge from the rental home. Housing options were so limited in Newton that W.T. began doubting the wisdom of this move. He'd uprooted his family so they could be homeless? Maybe it was time to head home to Arkansas and figure out their next move. But that was unacceptable to the good folks of Newton. Home economics teacher Sandra Love heard about the Johnstons' dilemma. She and her husband, Joe, had a solution.

Sort of.

Joe and Sandra had a one-bedroom trailer they used to store cow feed. The primary selling points were power, a working refrigerator, and a gas stove. A pull-out couch could fit in the cramped living area for the boys to sleep on. Yes, the Loves had to relocate some feed sacks to make room for the family, but if it kept W.T. from leaving Newton, it was a small inconvenience. Arrangements were made, although no one mentioned it to the current occupants of the trailer—several families of mice had moved in earlier.

While they were more than grateful for the generous offer of temporary housing, this was a little much even for a loyal coach's wife. Debbie was miserable. She was commuting to Beaumont to finish her degree in education, then coming home to wrangle two active boys who needed a lot more space than the small trailer provided. W.T. pitched in by getting Shaw to day care and Drew to school before heading to work. But that was getting wearisome too. Something had to give.

W.T. went to the local sheriff, who informed the house tenants they had sixty days to leave or face eviction. They took every day of that time frame before finally moving out, and the Johnstons bade adieu to the rodent families in mid-September. They were ready to settle down in Newton again.

6

A DIAMOND IN THE ROUGH

W.T. Johnston was in control again. After being promoted to defensive coordinator, he was a rising star in the high school coaching world, married to the love of his life, and the father of two fine sons.

Even a devastating loss proved invaluable for the future success of Johnston and the Eagles. Newton met the Sealy Tigers in the 1995 area play-offs. At the end of a long night at Sam Houston State's Bowers Stadium, the Eagles owned an ignominious record. Their 82–6 devastation at the hands of Sealy was the largest margin of defeat in Texas state play-off history at that time.

Even in that humiliation, the young coach saw something positive. Johnston was intrigued by the defensive formation Sealy used to throttle Newton that night. One of the unique competitive courtesies of Texas high school football is that rival coaching staffs willingly share offensive and defensive philosophies. During the off-season, the Sealy coaches graciously explained the workings of the Seven Diamond defense to the young assistant. He came home with the defensive principles that Newton runs to this day.

The Eagles won nine regular season games in both 1996 and 1997 before losing in the area play-off round both years.

During the off-season workouts in the summer of 1998, it looked as if the Newton Eagles could make a serious run at the state title. Coach Barbay was entering his twenty-fourth season, and even the ultra-realistic coach knew this could be a special group of kids. After dropping a disappointing 10–0 loss to larger classification powerhouse West Orange-Stark, the seniors decided they would not lose another game. Over the next eight regular season games, the Eagles piled up 365 points and gave up only 42. Led by dual threat quarterback David Walker and punishing running back Clifford Dean, the Eagles averaged more than forty points per game during the season. Dual threat wide receiver and safety Rod Gulley spearheaded a defense that surrendered only six points a contest.

Gulley remembers the rivalry game with Kirbyville that finished the regular season. "We decided to do something to make a statement. We ran to midfield, faced the Kirbyville sideline, and made some gestures and comments about the Wildcats."

Much to the surprise of the team, Coach Barbay did not react to the display. The senior-dominated team rolled to a 55–0 thrashing of their rivals and went to practice on Monday feeling pretty cocky about themselves and the upcoming play-offs.

Instead of prepping the team for the upcoming opponent, Coach Barbay explained to them how a Newton Eagle conducts himself between the white lines. He then proceeded to reinforce his point with a day of running nothing but sprints. Point made.

With attitudes and values properly aligned, the team roared through the play-offs. Wins over Liberty, Diboll, Rockdale, and Manor got them to the state semifinal game. The small-town heroes got a chance to play in a building once proclaimed the Eighth Wonder of the World.

Houston's Astrodome hosted the Newton matchup against Aransas Pass. A hard-fought 29–15 win put the Eagles in the state title game for the first time since 1974.

On December 19, the team bused to Nacogdoches to venerable Homer Bryce Stadium, the home of Stephen F. Austin State University. Newton would be playing for the 3A Division II Texas state title against the undefeated Daingerfield Tigers. Both teams could move the football, but Coach Barbay felt that Newton had the advantage with the defense led by Coach W.T. Johnston. "I said going into the game that our defense would win it for us," Barbay was quoted as saying later. He was right. Coach Johnston had borrowed and then refined a defense that stymied a Texas powerhouse.

Daingerfield was shut out and only gained 114 yards of total offense. Rod Gulley negated two scoring threats with interceptions. David Walker connected on two long passes that turned the tide offensively. Newton scored once before the half and put the game away with two second-half touchdowns. The Newton Eagles had their second state title and the first under Curtis Barbay. W.T. Johnston experienced the exhilaration of winning the ultimate title in Texas high school football.

7

SOMETHING IS TERRIBLY WRONG

Life was good. Johnston was a physical specimen, still able to get in the trenches with his players and more than hold his own. In 1998, the football piece of his life puzzle was perfect. His career was progressing right on schedule.

But something was wrong. By the time the long championship grind was over, Johnston was completely drained physically. He had never experienced anything close to this level of exhaustion. During the 1998 season, W.T. had a constant hacking cough and had trouble breathing. The doctor thought it was chronic bronchitis and prescribed steroids. With each dose, the drugs would make his symptoms better for a while. Then the cough and breathing difficulties would resurface.

Like too many men who grow up in a tough competitive culture, Johnston was unwilling to admit to Debbie how bad he felt and how much his breathing was diminished. He gutted it out, but by the end of the season, he couldn't climb up a set of stairs without stopping to rest. W.T. decided to see a doctor because it was affecting his ability to coach these kids he loved so much. Following the early pattern of his life, W.T. was making the right decision but for the wrong reason. Football was more important than being honest with his wife.

His longtime physician and friend Jimmie Bussey took a chest X-ray and went off to read the film as W.T. waited. Bussey returned with his head down, unable to make eye contact. Finally he blurted out, "W.T., you're sick."

"Tell me, what is it?"

"I don't know. I have never seen an X-ray like this. It could be cancer or AIDS or mesothelioma. I am sending you to a lung specialist."

Debbie was shocked and scared. "I had not been that concerned because he always dealt with sinus and bronchitis symptoms. I thought it might be pneumonia, but I had no idea it could be that serious. I also did not know that W.T. had kept it from me about how much his breathing had deteriorated during the football season. He confessed that he was afraid it was something like cancer, and he did not want to miss out on that special season."

W.T. considered his local doc's fears. He knew it wasn't AIDS, but the other two options seemed like a death sentence. For two weeks, W.T. anxiously waited to get an appointment with the specialist. When he finally got in, the doctor took a biopsy, and W.T. was told to call in a week to get the results. The doctor told W.T. that if he was unavailable, the nurse could relay the results.

Slow-forward one difficult week. Johnston called at ten o'clock in the morning, and sure enough, the doctor was not available.

"Tell me what you found out."

The nurse vacillated and finally replied, "I can't."

"But the doctor said you could let me know."

"He told me he needed to talk to you. Call back at 1 p.m."

At 1 p.m. it was the same story. The doctor was not available, and he had to be the one to give the report. W.T. remembers saying to himself, "This can't be good."

Finally, Johnston got through, and the doctor indelicately told him he had good news and bad news. "The good news is, you don't have cancer or mesothelioma."

After two weeks of agonizing over worst-case scenarios, that seemed like great news. "The bad news is you have sarcoidosis." W.T. still shakes his head over what he heard next. "I am prescribing you a massive dosage of prednisone. Your condition is manageable; you can research sarcoidosis on the internet."

As maddening as that phone-side manner might have been, W.T. and Debbie did just that. They discovered that sarcoidosis is an inflammatory disease that affects multiple organs in the body, but mostly the lungs and lymph glands. The X-ray that freaked out the local physician had shown the abnormal masses or nodules called granulomas in W.T.'s lungs. Ironically, the disease is seventeen times more likely to affect African Americans. W.T. was even color indifferent in his illnesses! This diagnosis seemed better than the other options because most patients can manage the disease. Yet it was sobering that this same disease took the lives of Hall of Fame football player Reggie White and comedian Bernie Mac.

Another bit of bad news was that W.T.'s stubbornness in admitting his illness had made things worse. The disease had progressed to stage 4. W.T. laughs when he confesses he didn't understand the severity at first. "That sounded pretty good because I thought they were on a ten-point scale. I didn't know there were only four stages." The advancement of the disease meant that eventually W.T. would have to undergo a double lung transplant. If only he had sought medical attention sooner, he might have been spared this difficult journey.

Another thing was gnawing at his gut. "I remember sitting in church and weeping. My pastor used to say that God would put rocks in your bed so you couldn't sleep if you weren't right with Him. I was beginning to understand that statement. I knew I wasn't right with God, but I still resisted."

During this spiritual crisis, a phone call came. W.T.'s mom had been involved in a serious car wreck, and he set out for Arkansas. To this day he has no idea why he did not choose the normal route to his parents' home. When Johnston selected the "scenic" back-roads path, the results were interesting, to say the least.

"It was like God was speaking to me all along the journey. I spotted a billboard I had not noticed before. It read, 'If You Die Today Are You Going to Heaven?' That was exactly what I was agonizing over on Sunday mornings."

God's sense of humor only became obvious to W.T. later. "I turned on the radio, and the only signal I could get in the middle of nowhere was a gospel-preaching station."

After turning the radio off, he spotted another billboard: "Do You Know Jesus?" "By the time I got to Hot Springs, I was wondering if I was going to be in worse shape than Mom." He knew the story of God's confronting the apostle Paul on his journey to Damascus, and it was literally W.T.'s "back road to Damascus" experience that God used to reveal his need. "I know in retrospect that was one more example of God preparing me for the next season of my life."

Still, Johnston could not pull the trigger to face his spiritual questions. At thirty-three, the carefully controlled life of William Theodore Johnston was beginning to unravel. He was a physical and spiritual wreck. He decided to fight one and fix the other.

8

THAT'S THE STUPIDEST THING I'VE EVER HEARD

Nothing seemed unusual about this summer Saturday morning. The peaceful tranquility of a country morning was punctuated by chirping birds and the excited barks of one of Debbie's rescue dogs chasing squirrels.

Debbie didn't think much about it when W.T. picked up the truck keys and announced he was going to talk to Tommy Walker. Walker's two sons had played for W.T. David Walker had just quarterbacked Newton to a state title.

His sudden need to talk to Walker seemed odd, but Debbie knew a lot of things had been troubling her husband. She suspected this conversation might be about more than football. It had been just a few months since his sobering diagnosis of sarcoidosis.

W.T. had decided to address his growing unsettledness in church. He was young, successful, and a real tough guy in a culture that rewarded that trait. He accepted that he was sick and maybe even sick to the point of death. But he was not afraid, because W.T. subscribed to the theory that tough guys take on challenges and don't back down.

Johnston held a common religious hope that if you are a good enough guy and do more positive than negative things, then God will look favorably on you when you die. The realization that his disease could eventually prove fatal caused him to seriously consider the prospect of eternity for the first time. W.T. thought it would be a good idea to talk about God, and he knew just the man to see. Tommy Walker was a no-nonsense preacher who would tell you the truth. If that was what W.T. was looking for that Saturday morning, he certainly got his money's worth.

Johnston told the preacher about his diagnosis and how serious it could be. He talked about his faithful churchgoing and how he was a decent and caring person. He loved his wife, his kids, and his players, and he hoped that would be good enough. W.T. told Tommy Walker that he knew he could die but he wasn't afraid.

Walker considered those words, then said, "That's the stupidest thing I've ever heard!"

Johnston remembers that moment as if it were just yesterday, and he remembers precisely the words that followed.

"W.T., you are going to Hell if you die now."

While that response might seem a bit indelicate, it was exactly the tone that resonated with W.T. Pastor Walker's direct words stung, but they got the attention of a coach who thought he could control everything with hard work and grit. Johnston was learning the sobering truth that illness and eternal destiny are things even the toughest guy can't control.

Walker explained the gospel to W.T. All men sin and fall short of God's holy standard. He showed through Scripture how God chose to do for us something we could never do for ourselves. He let W.T. know that no amount of good works could make us righteous and justified before God. Then the preacher told W.T. the Good News of the gospel and the miracle of grace. He showed W.T. in the Bible how God made a way for us to be declared righteous if we simply believe in faith that Jesus paid for our sins on the Cross. All W.T. had to do to receive this free gift of grace was to simply confess his need and sin and believe that Jesus is who He said He is.

Johnston was weighed down with conviction as the pastor detailed his lost condition. He had grown up in church and believed in God all his life, but he knew he was missing the mark. Yes, he was religious, but W.T. knew his regular church attendance was more about righting his father's wrong—his refusal to go to church—than worshiping God. Tommy Walker wasn't talking about religion. He was talking about a relationship with the living God, and W.T. knew he did not have that. He was comfortable with religion where he could pick and choose what he liked. Now he was being asked to do something totally out of character.

Give up control. Confess his weakness, sin, and need. God was asking the self-sufficient tough guy to bow down in humility and admit that he needed a Savior. W.T. couldn't do it.

As he headed home, W.T. was surprised to discover that several hours had gone by. He still had not made the decision to put his life and trust in Jesus. Giving up control scared him almost as much as Tommy Walker's dire assessment of his spiritual status.

When W.T. walked through the door, Debbie knew something significant was on his mind. He was unusually introspective, considering what Tommy Walker had told him. He knew he needed that assurance. But pride made one more assault to try to convince W.T. that he was okay without such a dramatic step.

The next Sunday morning, W.T. finally broke down and walked to the altar of Grace Bible Church, crying like a baby. He confessed his sin, pride, and stubborn independence, and his need for the saving grace of Jesus. Something remarkable washed over his soul that day, and he says it has never left him.

"Peace. The peace I received that morning is not explainable given my circumstances. God met me there and changed me that morning at that altar."

W.T. acknowledges that maturing in faith is a process.

"I still knew all my words," he chuckles. "And I could still twist off in anger. But something was different, and I knew it beyond a shadow of a doubt."

The surest test of real change is when those who know you best affirm it. Debbie Johnston was amazed. "The change was immediate. Teachers from the high school started telling me that W.T. was a different person."

W.T. couldn't believe it himself. "I was a grudge holder and hot tempered. Those things would still come out at times. But now I would immediately feel the conviction in my heart that I had done something wrong. I would seek to fix what I had said or done and ask forgiveness. I knew that conviction wasn't something natural or just my conscience speaking. This was something brand new, and I came to realize it was God's Spirit moving in my heart."

Something else changed dramatically with Johnston. He found something to be passionate about beside winning football games. Debbie noted that his new relationship with Jesus totally changed the way he coached.

"Before that day it was all about winning. The x's and o's are the easy part. Being a counselor, coach, dad, and mentor to these young men became my focus. I wanted to tell them about this miracle that happened in my life," Johnston recalls. "But mainly I wanted to show them what walking with God looks like. So many of these kids come from broken homes. Even their teachers don't know what they go through at home. But we get to spend so much time with them in a close relationship that we can learn more. Coaching can be a ministry for sure."

W.T. started a Fellowship of Christian Athletes chapter in Newton, and he soon saw up to two hundred kids attending every Friday morning at 5:30 a.m. Grace Bible Church hosted the meeting, and volunteers fixed breakfast for the kids. The coaches drove school buses and picked up kids on the scattered rural routes. Amazing things were happening, weaving a spiritual fabric throughout the entire community.

Grace Bible saw their attendance jump from sixty to more than two hundred people as this message of forgiveness was proclaimed. W.T. had found that his real calling in life was to share the Good News of the gospel through his gift as a coach and leader. What he didn't know was how much time God would give him.

9

THE NEW NORMAL

W.T. Johnston headed into a new football season with a new spiritual heart that helped him to accept his weakening lungs. With regular doses of heavy steroids, he was able to get back into the game with close to his usual vigor.

He was back in the town he loved, with a coach who was a Texas legend. Curtis Barbay mentored his willing pupil on everything from how to read a defense to why you should keep the floors clean in the workout room.

"I could go to him anytime to talk about anything," Johnston remembers. "He was a father figure to the kids, but also to the coaches. Most of us were not much older than the players. He was tough, but a wonderful and caring man. I have never had anyone who taught me more about football, life, and being a leader."

These lessons were being passed on by W.T. to a couple of young men living in the Johnston household. Drew and Shaw Johnston regularly attended practice, joined the coaches on the sideline, and heard the strategic discussions between the coaches. Football was their life, and both would wear the purple and white and play for their dad.

Drew inherited the fire to play and learn the game from his father. He never doubted that his career would also be spent inside the white lines. Drew had learned the "Eagle way" as a youngster playing Pee Wee and middle school football, and around the dinner table.

The Johnstons' eldest son had watched talented Newton teams fall short of the Texas holy grail from 1999 to 2003 during the grueling gauntlet of the play-offs.

During this time, Drew was lifting, running, studying, and preparing for his turn to wear the purple and white at Singletary Stadium. By 2004 he had developed into a hard-hitting and instinctive linebacker in his father's Seven Diamond defensive set. Not surprisingly, Drew became a coach on the field, calling signals and aligning his teammates to counter the rivals' offensive formation.

The 2004 Newton team got off to an uncharacteristically slow start with two losses in their first three contests. As the young players began to gel, the team began a ten-game winning streak. Coach Barbay's charges rolled through district play and the first three rounds of the play-offs. The state semifinal game became a bit of Texas trivia: It would be the last day that high school football would be played at the Houston Astrodome. Newton dispatched Brookshire Royal 49–12 to advance to another championship game.

Waco, Texas, was the setting for Newton's third title try. The Boyd Yellowjackets brought a spotless fifteen-win and no-loss record to the game. The first half was a standoff, but Boyd eventually prevailed and handed Newton its first loss in a title game.

Even by Newton standards, the expectations were high for the 2005 season, with lots of experience and some athletic difference makers. One of those athletes was a five-foot-eight dynamo who might have tipped the scales at 160 pounds with full football gear on. Toddrick Pendland was a remarkable story of tragedy and triumph. His disappointment at losing the championship the previous year fueled him to return and win for someone who was missing from his life.

Nine years earlier, Toddrick's mother, Tonya Ray Taylor, had sensed the imminent danger for her eight-year-old son and his younger brother Broddrick when their stepdad stormed home drunk and raging mad. She ordered Toddrick to grab his brother and hurry to the neighbor's house. Her last desperate word to her son remained indelibly seared into his memory.

"Run!"

Tonya Ray Taylor was shot and killed minutes later. Grandmother Mary Taylor gave the brothers a home and moved them to Newton Elementary School, where she worked. Uncle Tye Taylor got Toddrick into Pee Wee football and gave him something to take his mind off that terrible day.

Toddrick was always small, but by the time he arrived in high school, he ran with blazing and elusive speed. He would be an integral piece if Newton were to return to the championship game again. Toddrick wore a bracelet inscribed with his mom's selfless last word to remind him of her sacrifice and love. This season he would "Run" and dedicate each one to her.

Mother Nature almost denied Toddrick and the Newton Eagles their opportunity to even have a season. The team jumped to a 3 and 0 start, but literal dark clouds were on the horizon.

On September 24, 2005, one of the strongest hurricanes in Gulf Coast recorded history roared ashore at the bend where South Texas and Louisiana meet. Hurricane Rita was still a powerful Category 3 storm as it churned into Southeast Texas and followed the Neches River north toward Newton County.

BETWEEN THE WHITE LINES

Torrential rains and devastating winds topping out at 120 miles per hour damaged thousands of homes; Newton and the surrounding area were without power for weeks. School was canceled indefinitely as the community tried to put the pieces of their lives back together.

The Johnston family had evacuated to Hot Springs and stayed there for nearly two weeks. W.T. bought a travel trailer for the family to live in until power was restored in Newton and their house repaired.

"Imagine four not-so-small people crammed into a twenty-eight-foot trailer for two weeks!" Debbie recalls. Déjà vu. But at least they didn't have to share space with cattle feed and rodents this time. The Johnston home had a hole in the roof, a crushed carport and Suburban vehicle, and multiple downed trees. Many people in the area suffered far worse.

Coach Lidney Thompson's house was so damaged he was forced to sleep on a cot in his front yard and bathe in Lake Sam Rayburn.

When the players and coaches evacuated, W.T. had no idea where they had gone or when they planned to return. But one thing would always draw players, coaches, and residents inexorably back to Newton.

Football.

Soon after he returned to Newton, W.T. sat outside the field house wondering what would happen next. A group of volunteer power workers from San Antonio showed up. The workers asked where the power came into the field house. W.T. showed them the location.

The workers shook their heads. "This is the dangest place we have ever been to."

"Why is that?"

"Everybody in town wants the power turned on here first, so the boys can practice. They are more concerned about this field house than their own houses!"

W.T. smiled and shook his head. "Welcome to Newton, Texas."

The power was restored at the school, but another challenge faced the coaches. How could they reach the players to let them know practice was resuming? Local radio station KJAS was still on the air, and W.T. persuaded them to broadcast the practice times.

There was more than football at stake. In rural settings, it is difficult to get food and water to families in need, so the school provided a staging area to get MREs and bottled water to the community. Many residents had nothing to return to.

Running back Josh Alfred found his family home destroyed and was forced to move in with his grandmother. Many others shared similar stories.

The coaches gradually rounded up the troops, and football resumed three weeks after Rita's wrath hit Newton County.

"I thought there would be no more football," Alfred recalls. "But when we started practice, we were more determined than ever."

Wins over district foes Hardin and Kountze were followed by a Tuesday night win over West Hardin. The next week it was Monday Night Lights against Deweyville. Mother Nature intervened again as Newton won a lightning-shortened contest. The final regular season game (if you could call this bizarre year regular) was on a Friday against East Chambers. The Eagles had persevered through hell—and actual high waters—to post an undefeated district slate and berth in the state play-offs.

The Newton Eagles were more focused than ever as football became not only their passion but a healing force for the devastated community. The team did not face a significant challenge all the way through the quarterfinals. The semifinal opponent was the Comfort Bobcats. Newton punched their ticket to the championship with a convincing 63–34 triumph.

The championship game was scheduled at Tyler's Rose Stadium. It would be a battle of the Eagles—Newton and Argyle. It seemed only appropriate that Mother Nature made her presence known again with cold and drizzly weather on Friday, December 9.

Toddrick Pendland took a moment before the game to kneel and dedicate this game to his mom.

"This game was for her," Toddrick recalls. "And I never forgot that it was her concern for us, and not herself, that allowed me to even be here."

The night was extra special because his little brother Broddrick had been called up from junior varsity and shared the sideline with him.

It didn't take Pendland long to honor his mom with a touchdown run. Quarterback Darrell Jenkins scrambled and found a streaking Pendland for a fifty-one-yard touchdown pass on the opening drive. Later, Pendland would run twenty-three yards on a fourth and fifteen play to score. The first half was dominated by Newton. The defense shut out the Argyle Eagles. Linebacker Drew Johnston had already set a school record of 198 tackles coming into the title game, and he was adding to that total. Coach Curtis Barbay took a 28–0 lead into the locker room, but he knew that, like his own Eagles, Argyle would not quit.

Toddrick Pendland runs against Argyle in the State Title game.
(Courtesy Newtonsports.com/ Sherry Tracy)

Argyle quarterback Will Peyton led a comeback in the second half that saw them close the gap to just eight points in the fourth quarter. Now it was time for W.T. Johnston's defense to make a play, and they did . . . twice. In the final three minutes, one drive was thwarted when do-it-all star Toddrick Pendland broke up a fourth down pass. The last hurrah for Argyle ended on an interception by Newton defensive back Nicholas Adams.

Toddrick Pendland had done it for his mom, grandmother, uncle, brother, and teammates. The tiny scatback totaled 199 yards and scored three touchdowns.

"If Hurricane Rita couldn't stop us, nothing could stop us," Pendland told reporters. It was the first undefeated season in Newton football history and the second state title for Coach Barbay. W.T. and Drew Johnston experienced together the agony of losing that final game in 2004 and the sheer ecstasy of winning in 2005. They would never forget how arduous the path and how precious the opportunity is when you get there.

***W.T. and Drew share an
emotional moment after the
State Title game.***
(Courtesy Newtonsports.com/
Sherry Tracy)

10

LEARNING FROM A LEGEND

Not every coach is lucky enough to learn from a legend. Curtis Barbay was one of the most successful coaches in a state that is famous for great sideline leaders. W.T. drank in the wisdom from Barbay as he prepared for his day to be the man in charge.

W.T. recalls those days.

"You couldn't fool him. He was without a doubt the best x's and o's coach I have ever been around. A team would come out in a gimmick defense, and within one series he knew where everyone would line up and how to attack it. He always expected to win, and I took that attitude from him."

Perhaps the best things Johnston learned from his mentor were off the field. "We hardly ever had problems with parents because they knew that Coach

***Coach Curtis Barbay
diagrams a play.***
(Courtesy Newtonsports.com)

Barbay was always going to be fair. If you are fair with every single kid, you can coach them hard. He also let every kid know he was valuable. So many of these young men did not get that kind of message at home. We had kids with great ability and no confidence in themselves because they were demeaned at home. We had to believe for them and literally teach them to believe in themselves."

Another thing that W.T. learned from Barbay was when games are won.

"He taught me that games are won in preparation and at practice. Coach never believed that big rah-rah talks made a difference."

Looking back, W.T. chuckles at what he discovered about the short-term effect of pep talks. "The rah-rah goes bye-bye the first time you get punched in the mouth. Then you better have a plan to win."

Barbay and Johnston were honest with their players about each opponent. "We would tell them that if they played hard and followed the game plan, the game would be over at halftime. And we would tell them when a team had a chance to beat them and it would require extra focus and preparation. You can't lie to these kids. They know. When you lie about a few things, they start wondering how truthful you are about everything."

Success on the field continued as Coach Barbay piled up wins. The 2006 team lost in the regionals to Marlin and finished at eight wins and three losses. The 2007 season ended with nine wins and a quarterfinal loss to Tatum. Another quarterfinal loss to Daingerfield in 2008 capped a nine-win campaign. It was a special season for the Johnston family as youngest son Shaw started at offensive tackle for the Eagles. Debbie was amazed at how her boy changed between the white lines. "Shaw is a gentle giant off the field, but he was ferocious on it."

Shaw displayed the family grit when he suffered two transverse process fractures of his spine during two-a-day drills. He was in a great deal of pain and thought he might never get to play. The doctor ordered some time off and then told Shaw that playing was dependent on his pain tolerance. Not surprisingly, Shaw never missed a game.

Shaw remembers a teaching moment from his dad during his sophomore season that became one of his most valuable lessons later in life.

"We had lost a game on the road. The players were laughing it up, and there was horseplay on the bus coming home. Dad found out about it, and he was not happy. On Monday the coaches had us run 'airplanes' until we couldn't run anymore."

Airplanes are ten-yard sprints, hitting the ground, getting up, and running again.

Shaw remembers that day as if it were yesterday. "I was a big ol' lineman and not in as good of shape as some of the little guys. I was out of gas and struggling to keep going. All of a sudden, I hear the whistle behind me getting louder and louder as it got closer. It was my dad running with me, encouraging me, and telling me to keep going."

The significance of that moment only soaked in later. "Instead of just yelling at me, my dad came alongside and ran with me. It was a spiritual lesson in how he lived his life. He was showing me that you never quit trying, and when you get tired and discouraged, your Father is not off somewhere feeling angry at you. He is right there with you in the struggle."

As usual, Coach Johnston approached things selflessly. The team was consistently winning, and the Eagles were always a factor in the play-offs. People get used to winning and sometimes feel entitled. Even legends like Curtis Barbay can experience a bump in the road. "For all of his remarkable strengths, Coach Barbay was not a confrontational person," W.T. reflects. "He had announced that he would soon be retiring, and there began to be some divisions in the coaching staff about the future. I thought it would be best for Coach, the program, and me to move on. Plus I thought it would be fun to coach with my old friend Jack Alvarez at Kirbyville."

W.T. left the Eagles to become the defensive coordinator for the Wildcats in the 2009 season. He might have changed sidelines to coach one of the Eagles' rivals, but he and his family still lived in Newton. W.T. commuted eighteen miles to Kirbyville High School each day from his Newton home.

"At the time I had no idea how God would use that brief detour to grow my faith and prepare me for my journey ahead."

The Wildcats had an outstanding year with W.T. calling the defense and offensive coordinator Greg Neece sending in the offensive plays. W.T. drew close to Neece and developed great respect for his offensive mind. Kirbyville plowed through the regular season with only two losses. W.T. found himself across the field from his friend and mentor Curtis Barbay on November 6 when the Wildcats and Eagles met. It had to be a bittersweet moment for W.T. as Kirbyville prevailed 29–26 against a coach and players whom he loved. But between the white lines, you focus on beating your opponent, and W.T. did exactly that.

The Wildcats roared through the regular season and play-offs. Once again W.T. Johnston found himself in a state title game—but this time with Kirbyville. He was gaining a reputation as one of the best defensive coordinators in the Lone Star State. At Texas State University in San Marcos, the dream run for Kirbyville came up just short with a loss to Pilot Point.

Early in the 2010 season, Johnston again faced Coach Barbay when the Eagles came to Kirbyville.

"It was so strange to coach against the man who meant more to me than any man other than my father. I had run the dummy defense against the offense for so long that I had at least some advantage. We won by a pretty good margin."

The relationship between Barbay and Johnston had not frayed. "He knew why I left. The Newton program is bigger than one person, and I wanted it to be easier for him to finish out his incredible career."

Johnston returned home from a junior varsity game in late September to a message from Coach Barbay.

"You have to call Coach," Debbie urged W.T. "He said he wasn't feeling well."

W.T. knew that Coach Barbay rarely complained. Without hesitating, he went to visit his friend, who made an ominous statement.

"I am worried about this game," Barbay said.

W.T. didn't think the concern was for his opponent that week. "You are worried about Buna?"

"No, I'm worried about making it through the game."

Coach Barbay planned to go to the doctor on Monday, but he refused to miss the game. Johnston urged him to sit in the press box that Friday. Barbay declined with a stubbornness that W.T. Johnston could relate to.

The Friday night lights at Buna High School on September 24, 2010, seemed like so many others for Newton fans. The Eagles rushed out to a formidable lead over the hometown Cougars. The players returned to finish the task in the second half. Coach Barbay was the last to return to the sideline. He appeared to suffer a dizzy spell as he knelt near the goal line. Paramedics were called, and a hush fell over the stadium. An emergency vehicle arrived, and players, coaches, and fans prayed while Barbay was helped onto a stretcher and taken away. The game seemed surreal and almost meaningless as the Newton Eagles honored their fallen leader by holding on for a win.

Kirbyville was playing that night in Tyler, and W.T. got a call after the game. His dear friend Curtis Barbay was in trouble and had been taken to a Beaumont hospital. The next day, the early reports came in that Coach Barbay was doing a little better. W.T. and Debbie decided to go to Drew's game at McNeese State on Saturday and then head to the hospital in Beaumont on Sunday.

All day Saturday, the Johnstons monitored Barbay's condition. He seemed to be stable and on the road to recovery. They were making their way into McNeese State's Cowboy Stadium just before 7 p.m. when they received a shocking call. Barbay had suffered another setback and had died an hour earlier.

W.T. and Debbie sat in shock through the first half of the Cowboys game. Five players on the McNeese roster had played for Curtis Barbay. Should W.T. let those players know at halftime? Would it be better if they just found out after the game? W.T. decided to talk to McNeese coach Matt Viator. Viator felt that the players should know, and W.T. informed them in an emotional meeting before the second half.

As the news spread, the entire Newton community was shocked and heartbroken. Coach Barbay had invested forty-two years as a Newton coach, selflessly giving himself to grow young men into good football players and, more importantly, into good men. You could not find a person in Newton County who had not been touched by his life and influence.

The loss was devastating to W.T. In 1991, Coach Barbay had given a rough-edged kid from Arkansas a chance. When Barbay first brought him on board, there were no funds to pay W.T. until the fall term began, so Coach Barbay found him a part-time job.

"I remember racing home from work every day at 5 p.m., and Coach and I would go fishing. I probably learned as much on the lake as I did on the sideline from him. He was always giving to others, teaching those around him. He taught me more than any other coach I worked with. I cannot imagine how different my coaching career would have been without Coach's influence."

No church in Newton was large enough to hold the memorial service for a man who touched so many people. The home stands seat more than 1,500, and every seat was filled when the legendary coach made a final appearance between the white lines at Singletary Stadium. It was only appropriate that the fans of Newton and respectful fans of many other schools should gather at the place he loved so much. On Tuesday evening, September 28, his purple-draped casket was carried and accompanied by his players to the fifty-yard line.

Curtis Barbay had been head coach for thirty-six years. He finished with 317 wins, placing him fourth on the all-time wins list in Texas at that time. Remarkably, every single one of those wins was at Newton High School.

The players learned a tough lesson. Life goes on even when you don't want it to. They honored their revered coach with a *CB* decal on one side of their helmets, with the customary purple *N* on the other. The Eagles played well the rest of the season under interim coach Johnny Westbrook and found themselves once again in the play-offs. After an impressive first-round win over White Oak, the tumultuous 2010 season came to a disappointing end with an area round loss to Cameron Yoe. The Eagles players had honored their coach and heeded the words that would later adorn his monument at Singletary Stadium.

"Take pride in where you come from and do the best you can."

11

A TOUGH ACT TO FOLLOW

Newton fans had cheered only two head coaches for forty-two years. Lidney Thompson and Curtis Barbay had each delivered a state championship. The next hire would face enormous pressure to keep the Eagle tradition going; there is no tougher gig than following a legend. Just ask the coaches who followed John Wooden at UCLA or Vince Lombardi at Green Bay. Newton may be a smaller pond, but the heat is just as hot when you follow a coach like Curtis Barbay.

The school board recognized that continuity had been the key to success for Coach Barbay, who had adopted the offense of Lidney Thompson and refined it even more. The defense installed by W.T. Johnston was still in place. The players knew what to do on both sides of the ball; they had started learning those x's and o's in Pee Wee football. Clearly it made sense to keep the familiarity going. It was time to call W.T. in Kirbyville and bring him home for good.

W.T. remembers one thought going through his head again and again as he was introduced by the Newton school board as the new head coach.

Don't screw this up.

That would be unlikely. God had spent forty-five years preparing W.T. Johnston for this moment. Setbacks and serious illness had refined Johnston, along with observing and learning lessons from some extraordinary coaches. He had found peace and purpose through his commitment to Christ. He was ready.

He had learned so much from previous mentors, but his own life experience was a perfect fit for this diverse community. "I have coached with a lot of coaches who want the black kids to act white. You don't understand the culture if you try to do that. Here is the foundation of our program: The rules are exactly the same for everyone. If you follow our rules, we let you be who you are. If you can't do that as a coach at a diverse campus, then you can't succeed over the long haul."

Johnston also coupled the power of expectation with affirmation. "We coach the players hard. In fact, some of the boys who graduated have told me it is easier when they go to college programs than it was at Newton. When I chew on a player's backside in practice, I make sure I seek him out before he leaves the field house to put my arm around him and tell him I love him and believe in him. They can take the hard coaching when they know it is fair and that we care about them as men, not just football players. Recently I really got on a player. I texted him that night to remind him how much I cared about him."

For W.T., it has always been about team. "I am hard on the players gifted with great ability. But I understand that it is the blue-collar average athletes who win championships. When they are willing to do the work and execute what we ask of them, then the team works. There is nothing more beautiful to a coach than seeing eleven players acting as one to make a play successful."

W.T.'s first season at the helm saw the Eagles claim the 2011 district crown and advance to the play-offs. The Crockett Bulldogs ended

Newton's hopes in the second round, capping a nine-win and three-loss campaign.

The 2012 season left no doubt that W.T. could meet the Newton community's always high expectations. The Eagles raced through the regular season undefeated. After dismantling Teague, Grandview, and Franklin, the team was in the final four of 2A Division I. Only rival Cameron Yoe stood between Newton and another championship tilt.

The Eagles led 14–8 at the end of the first quarter. At halftime, the back-and-forth contest saw Cameron Yoe gain a slim 25–22 edge. A scoreless third quarter set up an exciting finish, but not for the Eagles. The Yoemen put up fourteen unanswered points and sent Newton home.

After two seasons, W.T. Johnston had a sparkling record of twenty-two wins and four losses. He was putting his own signature on the program while keeping the traditions that made Newton a special place to play football.

The future looked bright for the team, but there were dark clouds looming for W.T. Johnston.

12

A HOUSE DIVIDED CANNOT STAND

The 1998 sarcoidosis diagnosis had been a devastating blow. W.T. and Debbie were told there was an unknown amount of time before the insidious disease might force W.T. to have a double lung transplant in order to survive. He had managed to function with inhalers and heavy doses of steroids through the 2012 season.

The following year saw a change. W.T.'s lung capacity had diminished considerably, and he had to use an oxygen tank to make it through the practices and games. But his animated and forceful style on the sideline didn't change. The energetic coach wasn't hampered by this new reality, demonstrating to his players how you never quit giving your best. W.T. always kept a positive exterior, but it was becoming more and more apparent that he was experiencing considerable pain, on top of his breathing difficulties.

The team responded to his determined and inspirational leadership, finishing 2013 with another undefeated regular season. Would this year be when W.T. joined his mentors as a Newton head coach who made it to the ultimate game? The Eagles won the first two rounds and matched up with the White Oak Roughnecks in the semifinals. But Newton was not able to slow down the White Oak offense and fell by a score of 55–36.

Coach Johnston was devastated. He knew how tough it was to get to that final game, and he wasn't sure how many more chances he would get as the head coach.

The need for a lung transplant was becoming more apparent. W.T. had had an admittedly bad habit of using smokeless tobacco over the years. Doctors informed him he had to quit before he could go on the lung transplant list. He quit cold turkey with the help of handfuls of Jolly Rancher candies.

In February 2014, he was added to the lung transplant list at St. Luke's Health. The family knew the window of opportunity was small. If a suitable donor could not be found for W.T. soon, no one knew how much longer his lungs could last.

That life-and-death waiting game did not diminish the optimism Johnston felt as the 2014 football season began. He knew this football team had the potential to make the coveted journey to the title game that would be played at Arlington's AT&T Stadium.

But something seemed amiss during the summer workouts and preseason practice. Coach Johnston sensed that the players thought they were special simply because they had the Newton *N* on their helmets. Many teams viewed any game against Newton as their "play-off" game, and the Eagles always got their opponents' best shot. That meant the Newton players could not slack off. They seemed to be forgetting that it was hard work, team spirit, and family togetherness that made them Eagles. Johnston tried to communicate that he saw the team drifting off course, but those pleas weren't taken to heart.

W.T. was concerned about his squad, but his health was becoming more and more of a daily issue. His breathing continued to grow more labored, and he now required a larger oxygen canister wheeled at his side. W.T. recruited an eighth-grade football player named Darwin Barlow to be his oxygen caddy on the sideline.

Darwin remembers it well. "I was in middle school and I went to watch my cousin practice. Coach called me over and asked if I would help him with a job."

Just as a young W.T. had jumped at the chance to retrieve balls off a rooftop in order to be part of a team, Darwin wanted to experience the game from the sideline's unique point of view. "I got to see what the coaches see. It showed me what it is like to be in the arena from a different point of view."

W.T. knew he had made the right choice for the job. "Most kids would have wanted to sit with their friends at a Friday night game and not chase after a coach with a cart. But Darwin was a different kind of kid."

Darwin had another important responsibility—making sure his pockets were always full of Jolly Ranchers when W.T. asked for one. The coach and young player bonded in a way that could never have happened under normal circumstances. W.T. was teaching the eighth grader an important life lesson. "He showed me how he fought. I learned that when I face adversity, I can fight and not feel sorry for myself. Coach taught me that when it feels like it is just you and nobody else, you can always trust God."

The season opened on the road against 4A powerhouse Tatum, which would be a real

Darwin Barlow follows Coach Johnston with oxygen tank during 2014 season.
(Courtesy Newtonsports.com/Sherry Tracy)

test for the Eagles. They failed the test badly. Tatum rolled to a lopsided 39–7 win that wasn't even that close. A talented Newton offensive line was dominated by the Tatum defenders, and the Newton defense surrendered nearly four hundred yards.

With customary honesty, Coach Johnston summed up the performance tersely with reporters. "We really sucked out there."

Thankfully, one game does not define the journey. The ship seemed to be righted the following week with a thirty-one-point thrashing of Bridge City. Week three saw a return to undisciplined football as penalties, missed assignments, and fumbles led to a loss to Henderson. The next week saw more of the same as Orangefield High registered their first win over Newton since 1988. The once promising season teetered on the brink of disaster.

This Newton Eagles team was missing something more than just consistency. Coach Johnston had an idea that some (if not most) of the problem was off the field. He surmised that the parents and players were backbiting about who was playing and how much. He remembers discussing the team situation with the coaches. The words of Jesus came to mind that a house divided cannot stand. Abraham Lincoln included that Scripture verse in his acceptance speech as the Republican candidate for US Senate in 1858 against Democrat Stephen A. Douglas, who was pro-slavery. The question of slavery became a firebrand for the Civil War. Lincoln predicted the inevitable outcome of this struggle. "I do not expect the house to fall—but I do expect it will cease to be divided. It will become all one thing or all the other."

Coach Johnston knew his team would have to become all one thing or the other. They would choose either team or self. The season hung in the balance.

Johnston was asked by a local newspaper to comment about the slow start, and he agreed, with one unusual proviso. The sportswriter would have to write down everything W.T. said without any sugarcoating. *Beaumont Enterprise* sportswriter David Berry wrote what might have been one of the strangest story leads of his reporting career.

"W.T. Johnston is not good at keeping his opinions to himself."

Coach Johnston noted that this could be a good football team, but only if one thing happened. "The parents and fans need to quit talking to the players, and the players need to listen only to the coaches." In an era when leaders rarely rock the boat publicly, Coach Johnston called out the team, the parents, and the community in print. High school coaches around the state admired his courage and honesty.

"I probably got a hundred calls or texts from coaches applauding me and wishing they could get away with such comments," Johnston recalls with a laugh. "But Newton is a different place, and I knew that honesty would be respected."

On Friday morning, the weekly Quarterback Club meeting of boosters and parents was held. W.T. stood to address the group, knowing the article had been read by everyone in the room. He wasn't going to pull any punches now.

"I am the head coach of this football team. I make every decision for the good of this team and my boys. That is the way it is going to be. What I said in the paper this week is true. If you can't handle that, you need to get rid of me. Otherwise, that is the way it is going to be."

As Johnston sat down, the men and women in the room rose, giving him a standing ovation.

That night he shared some hard truths with the team in a rare pregame pep talk.

"Boys ... we need to come together. I don't know how much longer I will be your coach, but I promise you one thing. I am going to teach you to live until you die. And part of that lesson is that the people you can trust the most should be the people in this room. No one outside this locker room thinks you can win this game. We have never beaten West Orange-Stark. This season we haven't played like Newton Eagles. But tonight we start. We need to rise up as one if we are going to win. I want you to walk out of here with your arms locked together. We are going to go to midfield and circle with our backs to one another. When the rocks come at us, we will have each other's back and protect one another. Every time we need a big play, someone needs to rise up. When we need a stop, we need to rise up."

Newton fans were already a bit unsettled after the head coach called out the fans and players in the newspaper. And then ... instead of the usual energetic run out of the tunnel, the team purposely marched onto the field, arms locked together. Rather than breaking into offensive and defensive units, the teammates made a circle at midfield, back to back to back. It was clear this team was sending a message.

Eagle players locked arms to show solidarity.
(Courtesy Newtonsports.com/Sherry Tracy)

The game started, and Newton clearly had heard W.T.'s challenge. On third down plays, the defensive players would raise fists, signaling that they needed to rise up. After a big play, the rise-up signal was directed toward the sideline.

W.T. understood. "I don't think I have ever seen West Orange-Stark get handled like that physically." When time expired, the score read nineteen for Newton and seven for West Orange-Stark. The Mustangs could muster only forty-nine yards of total offense against the rejuvenated Eagles. At the end of the game, a triumphant Coach Johnston threw his arms in the air. His Eagles had indeed come together to rise up—the team's mantra for the rest of the season. At the end of the game, West Orange-Stark coach Cornel Thompson met W.T. at midfield and began making an animated point about a play that made him unhappy.

"I nearly passed out and had to sit down. Coach Thompson felt bad because he had no idea how sick I was."

W.T. Johnston had literally left everything on the field. His words and his actions continued to inspire the team. That game launched a remarkable run that helped keep W.T.'s mind off the increasing weariness, unrelenting pain, and compromised breathing he endured every day. He oversaw practice from a golf cart, zipping from spot to spot, giving him a chance to catch his breath. With that little reservoir of air he could coach each group as hard as ever.

Johnston received another bit of inspiration during this special season. He had become very close to both Greg Neece and his brother Doug during W.T.'s and Greg's tenure at Kirbyville. W.T. learned that Doug had been diagnosed with cancer and was being treated at MD Anderson Cancer Center in Houston. That began a special relationship with Doug that would inspire W.T. and show him how to trust God even more completely in a dark valley. "Doug was forty-two years old with four children. He was supposed to get better, and I

W.T. Johnston visits with Doug "Booty" Neece.
(Courtesy Debbie Johnston)

was supposed to be the one who wouldn't make it. I prayed that God would take me and spare him. Doug would finish every conversation the same way: 'Keep your eyes on the Cross, W.T.' Doug was the most godly man I have ever known, and he showed me what it looks like to praise God in the storm."

The Eagles finished the regular season with six straight wins and headed to the play-offs again. A magical turnaround from the "Rise Up" speech continued through the early play-offs. Newton dispatched New Waverly, Dublin, longtime rival Franklin, and Rogers. The Eagles had reached the final four once again, this time advancing with a convincing 48–21 win over the Blanco Panthers. In just four seasons, W.T. Johnston had gotten the team back to the state championship game.

But one unfortunate accident might have had a bigger impact on the game than anyone could imagine. During the semifinal game, Johnston suddenly charged after an official, and a startled Darwin Barlow could not keep up. The ten-foot oxygen tube became disconnected, and W.T. found himself on the ground, struggling to breathe. A panicked Barlow desperately tried to put his finger over the hole to keep the oxygen from escaping.

"Plug the dang thing back in!" Johnston gasped. Later he could joke about the incident with his characteristic laugh. "It's hard to argue with an official's bad call when you are flopping around on the ground like a fish out of water."

He was touched by how his team circled around him so fans in the stands could not see what was going on. Nonetheless, a fear was planted in his mind that would influence the usually unflappable coach as he prepared for the trip to AT&T Stadium.

"The game would be on Fox Sports, and I was scared to death that I was going to go down on national TV. I think that got in my head a little bit."

Johnston was in constant pain. Neither the players nor the fans knew how much agony he endured each day. His son Drew and the staff had some idea, but even they were not aware of his daily pain level.

Drew wanted this one for his dad. In the ultracompetitive world of Texas high school football, there might not be another chance. The opponent would be a Waskom Wildcats team that had dropped their opener and then reeled off fourteen wins in a row.

It was not a typical Newton performance. Waskom built a 20–8 lead at the half. The purple-clad Newton fans hoped for a second-half comeback. The Wildcats diminished that hope with fourteen unanswered third-quarter points. The offense sputtered, and the defense struggled to contain three talented Wildcat runners. Quarterback Trace Carter ran for seventy-two yards while running backs Kevin Johnson (eighty-seven yards) and the aptly named Junebug Johnson (ninety-one yards) shredded the usually stout Newton defenders.

Debbie Johnston had an uneasy feeling before the game. "I think that W.T. withdrew from his normally active role because he was afraid of collapsing on the field. That affected the boys. They look to W.T., and he was not himself."

No one can say whether a more proactive Coach Johnston would have made a difference against a very talented and worthy Waskom team. But W.T. did have a takeaway from his first championship game as a head coach.

Johnston determined that if God granted him another chance at the title, he would leave it all on the field. He just didn't know if he would be given enough time and the good fortune to try again. He had already experienced five trips to the ultimate game in Texas: three as an assistant at Newton, one as the defensive coordinator at Kirbyville, and now an appearance as a head coach. Many good coaches went their entire careers without getting to the ultimate game. W.T. wondered if his final opportunity would end with his being the runner-up. If that were the case, it would be okay. This had been a truly remarkable season that started in chaos and ended in unity.

W.T. Johnston had not realized the fears he felt on the day he took the job. He had not "screwed it up." He had kept the Purple Pride machine rolling at full speed with a sparkling record of forty-six and nine. Things looked good between the white lines. It was off the field that things were growing more and more dire.

13

THE VALLEY OF THE SHADOW OF DEATH

W.T. and Debbie Johnston began 2015 facing some very difficult questions. What would this year look like? Would a double lung donor be found? Would time run out before the call with news of a match came?

"Waiting for the call was bad. Even worse were the false alarms." W.T. and Debbie played an anxious waiting game as time counted down. W.T. knew the stakes better than anyone, yet he refused to feel sorry about his plight.

"I never asked why. I just never allowed myself to do that. Of course, I got down now and then. That's human. I knew that God had prepared me, and no matter what happened, He was going to use my testimony. God allowed this to happen, so I was at peace about what He would do. If I got new lungs, I would be grateful. If I died, then I was fixin' to get better because I know Jesus."

By March 2015, W.T. was near the end of the window that doctors felt was viable to survive the grueling double lung transplant surgery.

"By then I had gone through three false alarms at St. Luke's Hospital in Houston. Once I was called in, I got prepped, and then they told me the lungs were no good."

W.T. continued to show his players how to live until you die. One of the challenges of being on the transplant list is having to stay within four hours of the hospital. Johnston faced an emotional dilemma when he got word that his dad's health was failing, and that he probably should come to see him soon.

"I asked the doctors about going, but when I told them my dad was eight hours away, they said I couldn't go. They told me if the transplant call came and I was not close enough to get to the hospital, I would go back to the end of the line. I would be done if that happened."

Reluctantly, W.T. stayed home.

For one night.

The next morning, he woke up, and his son Shaw gave him the gentle nudge he needed. "Let's go see Papa," Shaw declared. Without hesitation, W.T. decided that Shaw was right. He had to do the right thing for his dad.

Minutes later Shaw was driving and W.T. was praying. "I had to see my dad. I knew God was in control, and if the call came while I was in Arkansas, then that would be what His will was for me."

When W.T. and Shaw arrived in Hot Springs, W.T. faced a couple of surprises as the family escorted him into a private room. The first surprise was that his dad only had a couple of days left after battling bladder cancer. The second was that no one had told Sonny or Lois how dire the situation had become. "I realized what all of that prayer had been about on the eight-hour drive. God was preparing me for this moment."

W.T. delivered the hard news to Sonny and Lois. As he sat by his dying dad's side, a lifetime of memories flooded through his mind. "I thought about how much I had longed for him to be with me in church when I was a young boy. He was my best friend, and I never understood why he didn't go to church with me. And now the only thing I could think about was how much I wanted to make sure I would see him again in Heaven."

W.T. asked his dad if he was okay with the Lord. Sonny didn't answer.

"I asked him again, and he expressed a need to be sure. My dad prayed with me and trusted Jesus on that hospital bed. My dad lived eighty-two years without knowing that peace and joy. I can't imagine living without that hope. I am so grateful I took the risk and went to see my dad."

The transplant call did not come while W.T. and Shaw were in Arkansas. Sonny passed away two days later with the peace that he was forgiven and his eternal destiny secured. W.T. did not risk leaving the Houston area to attend the funeral. It was hard to miss the funeral, but the younger Johnston knew he had made the trip that mattered, and now he had the hope of reuniting with his father one day.

As the days slipped by, W.T. was beginning to deal with the hard truth that he was at the two-minute warning on the transplant game clock. But God wasn't ready to welcome W.T. home quite yet.

"We got the call in April to come to St. Luke's," Debbie remembers. "You always hope for the best, but there was that nagging memory of false alarms."

This time the lungs were deemed good. W.T. was prepped and wheeled into surgery on Thursday, April 9. Doctors were completely candid with Debbie and W.T. about the risk of this procedure. It definitely gave W.T. pause.

"There was a fifty-fifty chance of me not getting off that table. My family left, and they wheeled me into the operating room. That's when it got real and scary. It was just me on that table with the doctors. The first thing they did was secure my feet. Then they stretched my arms out to my sides and secured each arm. All I could think of was that I was in the same posture as Jesus on the Cross. As the medical personnel prepared me for surgery, I was begging Jesus to save my physical life. I thought about how I always ask God for help when I'm in trouble. But when things are good, what do I do for Him? Jesus suffered pain and death for me without flinching. Thinking of what Jesus willingly did for me on that Cross gave me supernatural peace to trust Him with my fear. At that moment, I believed that no matter where I woke up, things would be fine. Either I would have new lungs and a chance to keep doing what I loved, or I would have a new home in Heaven with the Lord I loved. I was ready either way."

A double lung transplant is an extremely difficult surgery and can take up to twelve hours. Debbie received regular updates throughout the surgery. She was more than a little freaked out when she learned the lungs had not arrived when expected and her husband's chest had already been opened in preparation for the transplant. The lungs finally arrived, and the first one was put in about four hours after Johnston had been wheeled back to the operating room, followed by the second. The entire process took about nine hours. People from Texas, Arkansas, and other places around the country prayed and anxiously awaited the news.

When W.T. woke up in Houston instead of Heaven, they were all relieved. A new set of lungs now gave him hope that his long and difficult ordeal might finally be turning a corner.

W.T. and Debbie had been warned that the major risk of a lung transplant is rejection. The body sees the donor organ as a foreign object, triggering the immune system to attack the new lungs as if they are a disease. Massive doses of immunosuppressants are given to the recipient to prevent rejection, but that comes with its own risks. Since the drugs work by limiting the immune response, they correspondingly raise the risk of infections and can make normally routine illnesses life threatening. Although it would still be a difficult journey to get back to the sideline, that was exactly where W.T. wanted to be.

The transplant team at the hospital required that any patient who lived more than two hours away stay in Houston in case any complications arose. The Johnstons looked for temporary housing. In the immortal words of Yogi Berra, it was "déjà vu all over again." Debbie found herself living in an RV trailer in Houston, possibly for the next three months.

"W.T. only stayed in the hospital for twelve days before being released," Debbie remembers. "The first four weeks of his recovery in the RV went amazingly well. The doctors were so pleased, they were discussing letting us go home to Newton on weekends."

Exactly one day after the four-week checkup, W.T. began to suffer stomach pain, nausea, and diarrhea. The doctors readmitted him and were able to get his stomach issues under control.

One week later, his symptoms returned with much greater severity. His pain increased, the diarrhea was constant, and he was fading quickly.

The doctors were puzzled and began running test after test. They hoped it was a reaction to the medication, but that was ruled out. W.T. was losing weight and strength at an alarming rate, and no one knew why. Once again, time was running out for W.T. Johnston.

14

A MYSTERIOUS VISITOR

W.T. Johnston was dying. For the first time since he was diagnosed with sarcoidosis, he was ready to give up.

Now down to a scant 140 pounds, the once robust coach was wasting away. Few people knew how much pain he lived with every day. Doctors faced a growing frustration as Johnston spiraled downward. After the months of agony and false alarms, this latest setback seemed so unfair when just five weeks earlier the transplant looked like a success.

But the truth is that if life were fair, W.T. Johnston would have been in the weight room with his players instead of hooked up to IVs and monitors. The upcoming season for the Newton Eagles was full of promise, and the veteran coach believed it could culminate with that elusive state title. More than anything, he wanted to be a part of that. But instead of plotting football formations, the fifty-year-old coach found himself fighting for his life. The disconcerting beeps in the intensive care unit were a constant reminder as W.T. drifted in and out of consciousness.

The hope at this point was only for survival, and doctors prepared Johnston for a life apart from the high stress of Texas high school football coaching. Johnston had begged the doctors to let him go home and die. He certainly did not want to pass away in a sterile hospital room away from everything that gave him reason to live.

People across the community, county, state, and country were praying. Debbie could feel that, even as she wondered if those prayers were simply preparing her husband to pass into the presence of God. This time W.T truly was ready to die. He wasn't anxious. He was confident that he was right with God. Yes, he would enjoy teaching his grandson Jax to love fishing, hunting, and football. And he hated the thought of leaving Debbie widowed at such a young age. He grieved at the thought of no more time between the white lines, teaching young men how to believe in themselves and the power of teamwork. Despite all that he had to live for, he could not bear the relentless pain anymore.

Debbie was more concerned than ever. "I had never seen W.T. give up. I was praying for something—anything—to give him hope."

And then, in the darkest moments of this storm, a mysterious visitor showed up in his hospital room. W.T. remembers that he was an older black man dressed in khaki pants, a long-sleeved tan shirt, and gleaming, polished brown shoes. There was a gray patch in his neatly groomed black hair. The man's smile lit up the room, and his presence brought W.T. comfort—he longed for another visit.

It happened the following day. When the man arrived, Johnston barely had enough strength between his gasps for air to ask his guest, "Where have you been?"

"Making my rounds, Son," the man said with a captivating smile. "Making my rounds." W. T. invited his engaging company to sit down, and for a little while they talked football and life. The visitor told W.T., "You are going to live. Quit worrying."

The man returned the next day and the next. Each day, the unnamed caller would end their visit with these parting words before he left the room. "Don't worry, Son," he would say with conviction. "You are going to be okay."

W.T. hated when the man left—he wanted to go with him. The visits broke up the cacophony of intensive care with peaceful assurance and lasting encouragement.

W.T. Johnston may have wanted to end the pain, but his new friend's presence kept him going while the doctors continued to search for answers.

Back in Newton, another miracle of encouragement was in the works. Kristi Staley had known the Johnstons since the early 1990s and had worked with W.T. as an administrative assistant for most of that time. "We were raising money among the staff, but we wanted to do something more. We had seen a lip sync video on the internet, and we thought that would be fun. Coach Barbay's grandson Brady was home from college. He was talented in shooting and editing videos, and he agreed to help."

The students and staff got to work making signs to encourage Coach Johnston as well as printing a giant head shot of him for the video. The group decided to use "Best Day of My Life" by American Authors as the sound track. When everything was ready to film, Brady moved his camera through a sea of enthusiastic students in the halls and classrooms of Newton High. Students, athletes, teachers, and administrators enthusiastically lip-synced to the song and danced with their signs and the coach's "big head" held high. The camera continued to a pep rally and then to the field house, where W.T.'s players showed their affection and respect for their coach with smiles, signs, and gestures. W.T.'s son Drew and grandson Jax made a cameo appearance as the video ended in Singletary Stadium, with the entire student body spelling out "COACH" between those esteemed white lines. The production was a professional and powerful message advocating the need for transplant donors and showing W.T. and his family how much the school loved them.

Debbie was at the hospital when the phone rang. It was Kristi Staley, urging her to share the video with W.T. right away. Debbie had no idea the school was shooting a video, but from the excitement in Kristi's voice, she knew it must be special.

"I remember getting frustrated because I was having a hard time getting it downloaded in the hospital. I finally got to see it and share it with W.T. We laughed and wept as we watched this amazing demonstration of love for us. They must have taken an entire school day to produce it. Without a doubt, that video proved to be one of the turning points for W.T.'s spirits."

In a letter to the students, W.T. expressed how much their selfless gift meant to him. "This video is the best medicine I have received! It is unbelievable how much time and effort you have put into this for me. I really appreciate it, and I don't know how I can ever repay you. I don't have the words."

Repayment was not expected. The students and staff were thrilled to do something that showed how much they appreciated Coach Johnston.

The community of Newton showed its love in other tangible ways. Kristi Staley recalls the plan. "We knew that the family was running up lots of charges having to live away from home. We asked a local bank to set up an account and issue a debit card for W.T. and Debbie. The account was funded just by word of mouth throughout town."

The fund-raising for the family became a modern-day version of what happened in *It's a Wonderful Life*. Just as the people of Bedford Falls dumped money on a table at George Bailey's house, the folks in Newton deposited whatever funds they could into the Johnstons' bank account. Debbie was deeply moved.

"Every time we checked the account or needed money, there was a balance in the account. Newton is not a wealthy community. This is just an example of good people helping one another. We were so grateful for the support."

W.T. still marvels at this community's generosity. "There is no way I can pay back the people of Newton for what they've done for me. This is not some wealthy suburb in Houston. These are people sacrificing their own wants and needs to help me. There is just no way I can express the gratitude I have for them. It's just such a special place to coach."

Both the uplifting video and the love of the community helped bolster W.T.'s hope. More Heaven-sent gifts, just like the faithful visits in the hospital from the unidentified man.

W.T tried repeatedly to find anyone who could identify the man so he could thank him. No one had seen anyone who fit the gentleman's description either in W.T.'s room or anywhere else in the hospital. W.T. was certain the stranger came every day to boost his lagging spirit.

The hard-charging football coach might be the last to believe he was "touched by an angel," but that is exactly what he believes now. He was ready to die until this visitor assured him it would all be okay. His face and gentle smile were burned into W.T.'s memory, and the feeling of peace the man always left behind was inexplicable. Call it what you like. W.T. Johnston is convinced God sent an angel of encouragement to give him the strength to hang on.

Doctors kept him nourished intravenously as they frantically searched for answers. They decided to try massive doses of steroids, and that regimen began to help. W.T.'s nausea eased, and he began to put weight on instead of losing it. After three agonizing weeks, he was released. But once again things didn't go easily for Johnston. He broke out in a persistent rash that added to his misery. Doctors did a biopsy just to make sure it wasn't a rare complication.

It was.

The medical staff can be forgiven for not finding the cause sooner, since up to that time only four known cases of such a complication after an organ transplant had been identified in the United States and just sixteen in the world.

Johnston was deathly ill with Graft Versus Host Disease (GvHD), a rare immune reaction after lung or other organ transplants. The reaction is more common with bone marrow procedures.

In W.T.'s case, the disease was causing the white blood cells that came with his new lungs to attack his body. When W.T. was diagnosed, the longest a patient with GvHD had lived was 280 days, less than a year. To be honest, the Johnstons might have taken that time frame, given how dire his current situation was. At that moment, they wondered if he would even make it home again.

W.T.'s doctors at St. Luke's knew about an experimental protocol being implemented at MD Anderson. W.T. was on board with being a guinea pig. "Why not? If the treatments helped me, that would be great. If not, at least others might be helped down the road."

To fight the attacking white blood cells, doctors at MD Anderson injected a drug called methoxsalen into Johnston's blood. The naturally occurring drug comes from bishop's weed, an herb cultivated by the ancient Egyptians. The blood was then cycled through a process called extracorporeal photopheresis (ECP) and went through UVA irradiation before being returned to his body.

The unusual procedure stopped the progression of GvHD, and for six months Johnston made a weekly pilgrimage to Houston for treatments. After that, for an additional six months, he was monitored and treated every two weeks.

W.T. was still a shell of his former robust self. Doctors demanded he wear a surgical mask at all times to avoid a deadly infection. And worst of all, they had told him he should never coach again. W.T. just asked folks to pray for the doctors, and then he and God would work out the coaching thing.

15

LIVE 'TIL YOU DIE

Telling W.T. Johnston that he couldn't return to the football field was as effective as telling a golden retriever not to wag his tail when greeting someone.

"Those kids were my best medicine. They made me laugh. I needed to be around them to recover."

Michelle Barrow, the superintendent of the Newton Independent School District, was understandably reluctant to allow Coach Johnston back on the sideline. Was this really the best thing for him? Shouldn't he be resting and regaining strength instead of subjecting himself to the stress of coaching? What if he died during a game, in front of the kids and fans?

W.T. Johnston knew that was a possibility. But the determined coach negotiated a way to be near his team. Superintendent Barrow agreed to let him coach if he stayed on a golf cart behind the team's benches. He was still an integral part of the game, tethered via headsets to the other coaches and the press box, allowing him to weigh in on the plays. Following doctors' orders, Johnston wore a surgical mask to protect his compromised immune system.

**W.T. Johnston coaching
from his golf cart.**
(Courtesy Newtonsports.com/
Sherry Tracy)

"I only have vague recollections from some of the games and none from others," Johnston recalls, laughing. "I hope I said the right thing when they asked for my input. I just can't remember. I might have told them to punt on first down."

The 2015 season was a confusing blend of football plays and hospital treatments.

During weekly practice, Johnston roamed up and down the field in his golf cart. He had told his players about his disease and its likely outcome. "I told them that I was going to teach them football, but I was also going to teach them something more important. How to live until you die."

W.T.'s friend Doug "Booty" Neece was doing the same thing with his family. Doug had coached his three oldest boys before his cancer diagnosis. At the end of the 2104 season, he had been hospitalized at the state high school championships. Now, he had just watched his son Drew play for Albany in the 2A title game, which the Lions lost by seven to Bremond. Newton was slated to take the field next, and Doug planned to stay and watch his friend's team. By halftime he was feeling bad, and the family took him to a Dallas hospital, where he stayed for two weeks. His prognosis was again unclear.

W.T. watched his friend navigate bad news with upbeat trust in God. Johnston mixed that same message into practices and games.

"I always want to make sure the players are okay spiritually. We will all face life. The question will be, how do you handle what life throws at you? Who will you lean on? I didn't learn until later in my life that there is much more to life than football. It took some hard knocks to teach me. I hope I can have an impact on my kids, so they don't have to learn the hard way. But if they do have to learn that way, maybe something I said will come back to them to help."

One thing has been consistent with W.T. for every step of his journey with Jesus.

"If there is something that you cannot control, don't worry about it. Put it in God's hands and trust Him. Don't question why. Lean on Jesus. Trusting gets easier the longer you go through a storm. Lean on Him when you don't know where to turn."

Longtime friend Mike Tankersly marvels at W.T.'s consistent approach in his faith walk. "Through all the pain, setbacks, and adversity this man has gone through, I have never, not one single time, heard him ask why. It's remarkable."

W.T. had another unwavering message to impress on his team. "I tell the kids that there is no place for prejudice between the white lines or outside them. I have seen white people who are prejudiced. I have seen black people who are prejudiced. Here is what I tell them: 'Don't have anything to do with any of them if they are dividing people by color.'"

It was difficult to coach from a cart. The players did not have that familiar and animated presence shoulder to shoulder with them on the sideline. Newton won their first game, and then an almost unthinkable thing happened. The Eagles lost the next four in a row. But the lessons drilled into those young men over many years resurfaced. There is no quit when you put on the helmet with the *N* emblazoned on the side.

The team rolled through district matchups and into the play-offs once again. Newton sent Buffalo home, effectively retaining their remarkable streak of never losing a first-round play-off game under any coach. The Eagles defeated Marlin soundly in the second round but lost a tough and close battle with Franklin.

With the team gelling during the season and many key starters returning, Newton shaped up as a favorite to make it back to the title game in 2016.

Coach Johnston had a positive development too. The medical team determined his stomach issues were due in large part to a failing gallbladder, another side effect of the brutal transplant surgery. When his gallbladder was removed, he began to put on weight and regained a lot of his vigor.

After his nearly dying and then persevering through a disconnected season of coaching "à la cart," it looked as if everything could come together in 2016. Johnston's goal remained the same it had always been and would continue to be for every day God gave him: to teach each of his players and every person around him how to live until you die.

16

BACK IN THE SADDLE AGAIN

To the surprise of his doctors, Coach Johnston was back on the sideline coaching. Initially, when he was diagnosed with GvHD, W.T. asked the doctors how much time he had.

"We have no idea," the medical team admitted. "There isn't enough data to even foster a guess."

Johnston journeyed to MD Anderson for a one-year checkup with transplant specialist Amin Alousi. With a twinkle in his eye, W.T. asked the doctor a question.

"Did you ever think we would be having this appointment?"

"Honestly, no," Dr. Alousi replied. "We have only found four cases, and you are the only one who has this longevity. There is no reason for you to be here."

"Why do you think I'm here?"

"Because of me?" Dr. Alousi said, with a smile.

W.T. begged to differ. "Nope. Because people were praying. I know I have the best doctors in the world, but the reason I am here today is because of the prayers of so many people."

BETWEEN THE WHITE LINES

Johnston had regained most of his weight and was able to shed the ever-present oxygen tank. In fact, Darwin Barlow, his oxygen caddy from two years earlier, was now a highly touted running back for the Eagles. The team had seven offensive starters returning and nine on the defensive side. W.T. was able to coach the boys hard in preseason and practice. Newton rolled into the play-offs with an undefeated record.

In 2015 W.T.'s friend Doug Neece had rallied from his cancer treatments, and it had looked as if he might have a chance to defeat his cancer. Doug had been a fixture at his older boys' regular season football games for the Albany Lions. He had hung on long enough to coach his youngest son, Bennett, just as he had coached Bennett's older brothers. Drew Neece was the Albany quarterback, and his brother Jax played defense.

As the Lions headed back to the play-offs, Doug had takentook a turn for the worse and was hospitalized. When W.T. talked to him, Doug told his friend he only had a few days left. His voice was weak, but his message was strong. "Keep your eyes on the Cross." Those final words replayed over and over in W.T.'s mind as the Eagles continued moving forward in the 2016 play-offs. On Friday afternoon, November 13, 2015, Doug "Booty" Neece had lost his battle. That same night, Drew threw five scoring passes and Jax led the defense to an emotional 54–17 win over Haskell.

W.T. kept wondering why he was given more time and Doug Neece was not. But the message from his friend would not leave him. When adversity strikes, keep your eyes on the Cross.

Newton's first play-off opponent was a familiar one. The Waskom Wildcats had crushed the dreams of the Eagles in the state championship two years earlier. Newton's revenge was to crush Waskom 66–0. Buffalo was dispatched in round two 50–7. The Elysian Fields Yellowjackets were not intimidated by the Eagles' early-round domination. In their game, the score was knotted 20–20 after three quarters. Newton's defense stepped up, and the offense mustered a field goal and touchdown for the Eagles to escape with a 30–20 win.

Once again, the stage was set to play for a championship. Only the Arp Tigers stood between the Eagles and the journey to AT&T Stadium in Arlington.

Arp was dominating defensively, and the Eagles made uncharacteristic mistakes. A dropped touchdown pass and untimely penalties helped put Newton in a 13–0 hole late in the fourth quarter. The Eagles punched in a touchdown with just over a minute left. This season came down to an onside kick attempt. As they had the rest of the evening, Newton came close but could not recover. Arp ran out the clock on a huge upset.

"Sometimes it's not meant to be," W.T. reflected afterward. "They outplayed us. That's all you can say. They were ready to play, and we just came out flat. We just didn't play very well tonight. We fumbled at a crucial time, we dropped touchdown passes—that's part of it. And Arp is a good ball club; they'll probably win the state title."

This one hurt. W.T. knew when a team had the right stuff, and this group of players should have been in the championship. The result also reiterated what a difficult grind it is to get to that final game. As usual, the Eagles would field a strong team the next season. Once again W.T. Johnston wondered if he would ever see that elusive title of state championship coach added after his name like his predecessors Thompson and Barbay. Whether time would allow it to happen or not, W.T. definitely knew some changes needed to be made.

17

LAST CHANCE?

Over the next few weeks, W.T. reflected on the disappointing finale in 2016. The march to the final game in football-crazed Texas is demanding and sometimes requires a lucky bounce or two. W.T. had learned not to worry about things he couldn't control but to always pay attention to the things he could control. One of those things was making sure he had the right people around him.

During his two-year stint in Kirbyville, Johnston had been blown away by Greg Neece's offensive mind and play calling. They had bonded as coaches who held the same values and grown to be like brothers through Doug Neece's cancer journey. Greg had been on the coaching staff at Kirbyville for twelve years—six of them as athletic director and head coach. After the 2016 season, he was feeling unsettled. Greg had a good situation in Kirbyville, and it was a good program. Yet something was driving him to make a change. He talked to his wife, Michelle, about his desire, and she was supportive and encouraging.

In March of 2017, Greg Neece made an announcement that made no sense to reporters or the scores of "experts" on social media. He had accepted a job as the quarterback coach at Newton High School.

The media hubbub was immediate and loud. "Financially it made no sense. Career wise it made no sense. But personally and spiritually it made all the sense in the world," Neece said. The people closest to him were also thrown for a loop. When they asked why, Greg gave them his simple answer.

"I wanted to coach with my friend."

He simply trusted God that being in Newton with W.T. was the right thing to do. Meanwhile, some talks were happening just up Highway 190 in Jasper. Darrell Barbay, son of the Newton legend, was the head coach for the Jasper Bulldogs. Younger brother Bryan had been a steadying influence for the Newton Eagles as an interim head coach and offensive coordinator while W.T. was recovering his strength. With Johnston back on the Newton sideline, Bryan decided to join his brother to become the offensive coordinator at Jasper.

That opened the door for Greg Neece to become the offensive coordinator at Newton. His step of faith to be a part of the Newton program had worked out. W.T brought a couple of other familiar faces over from Kirbyville. Coach Steve Fentress joined the Eagles to coach the offensive line, and former Kirbyville quarterback Kael Jones also joined the staff as the new quarterback coach.

Neece was happy to be with W.T. Johnston again. "He told me that he brought me in to score points and I didn't need to worry about anything else. That is a fun job description for an offensive coordinator."

It also gave Greg quality time with this remarkable mentor. "I have met some really tough men in my life that I have admired. My brother was tough. This is a profession full of men that are tough. But I would probably say that W.T. Johnston is the toughest guy I have ever known. I wanted to learn more from him about this Newton phenomenon. There is no place like it that I have ever seen. I watched him push kids to the limit and get on them hard on the field. Then he would bring them into his office to encourage, hug, and even pray with them. Coach feels like we are given this gift of coaching to build complete men and not just teach *x*'s and *o*'s. How could you not want to be a part of that?"

The Eagles' coaching roster was fully staffed. Greg Neece would call the offensive plays from the press box while Drew Johnston would fire up the defense from the sideline. Everything was in place for what Drew feared might be the final shot for his dad to get a championship ring as the Newton head coach.

Summer practice and preseason camp were all business as the team focused on the task ahead. Newton is not a place where a district title or a play-off win or two get you a pat on the back. The folks in this town circle their calendars for a trip to the state title game every year. It's a major disappointment when that can't be marked off everyone's to-do list. W.T. would not have it any other way.

"I couldn't coach at a place where a six and four record is good enough. I love being with a team that has a target on its back."

The preseason workouts looked promising. One player was completely focused as he approached the season. He had reason to be focused and was grateful for this chance. Always a gifted athlete, Corbin Foster had endured his own litany of setbacks.

"In eighth grade I tore up my shoulder. I healed from that and was ready to go as a freshman. That year I tore my ACL and MCL in my knee. Coach Johnston called or talked to me every day. He had a special rehab workout developed for me. He was my rock and my encourager."

Corbin did the work and was set for his varsity debut as a sophomore. It was not to be. "I tore the ACL in my other knee, and I was out another year. Coach was there again. He pulled out his workout sheet and encouraged me to keep going. He told me his story, and I realized that if he could look death in the eye and come back, I could do this. He sets the tone for all of us. Hard work, perseverance, and faith."

W.T. reminded Corbin that God works in ways you can't always see at first, and his player began to understand.

"I turned to God in this hard time. I felt like it might never happen for me to live out my dream on the field. Coach said, 'Maybe you are going to Beaumont Orthopedic because you were supposed to meet Dr. Gene Isabell.' Dr. Isabell inspired me to think about being a surgeon someday. God always makes things work out for good. Now my goal is to go to medical school and help others."

The Eagles finally had their defensive leader Corbin Foster healthy and primed for a great season. There was an abundance of speed, talent, and aggressiveness. They had the players in place to execute the Seven Diamond defense, and they knew it could be a special year.

"We play the same defense the Chicago Bears played back in their Super Bowl year in 1985," Drew explains. "It can be a four-man front or a three-man front. We put skill people at defensive end and even tackle so they can drop and cover if needed. You know we have some speed on the line when we have players with running back numbers up there."

Evander Williams was a good example of that philosophy. Number 22 was listed as a running back/defensive tackle. He was strong, physical, fast, and a little chatty with opponents. Taderaun Seastrunk was another undersized but athletic defensive tackle. Another former running back on the defensive line, Bryson Thomas, wore number 6. Opponents weren't used to linemen who were as fast as some of their skill players. Nose guard Kristian Paulette weighed in under two hundred but was a fierce tackler and presence in the middle along with junior Galen Kellum. Senior Jadrian McGraw started for the third year at defensive end. On the other side, rising sophomore star James Sylvester packed 240 pounds on his six-foot-five frame. Colleges from all over the country were keeping an eye on him.

Linebacker Maliak Metoyer loved to fly around the field and pursue. Davien Johnson was a solid and dependable defensive and offensive player known as the "Swiss Army Knife." Free safety Zach Gulley was a Newton legacy athlete in the defensive backfield. His dad, Rod, had played for W.T. as a part of the championship team in 1998. Newton was unusual among small schools because only two full-time defensive starters were two-way players. Quarterback Josh Foster and wide receiver Taumazia Brown were the free safety and shutdown cornerback, respectively. Drew Johnston would also be counting on contributions from Dominique Seastrunk and Seth Craft. He knew this defense could be a football version of *The Fast and the Furious*.

Even with all of this talent, there was something eating away at Drew. He feared he would be the one who kept his dad from a championship ring by making a bad call or being poorly prepared. Drew was determined to not let that happen.

Coach Greg Neece also had some burners to work with on the offensive side. Quarterback Josh Foster and running back Darwin Barlow had already committed to play Big 12 football at Texas Christian University. Wide receiver Taumazia Brown was one of the top-rated pass catchers and defensive backs in Texas.

And then there was running back Kevin Watson, another Newton legacy player, following his dad, Kevin Sr., who was also a member of W.T.'s '98 title team. "Kevin is old-school Newton," W.T. says proudly. "Not as fast as some of the others, but he is dependable and one of our main guys. You build championships on guys like Kevin. He is always smiling and always bringing it for the team."

Noah Williams always brings a smile to W.T.'s face. "We didn't use him enough as a junior, and that is going to change. He is tall and fast and has a world of talent. The only problem is getting him to believe in his ability. Well, to be honest, there is one other problem. He drives me crazy at practice. But in a game, he produces. He is a great downfield blocker and is as tough as they come."

Johnston points out one more distinction Noah holds. "He might have the record for the most butt chewings from this head coach! But I give him credit. He can take it and learn from it. He knows how good I think he can be, and that is why I push him. He also knows how much I love him."

Another skill player that the offense would depend on was Davien Johnson. Tight end Lakendrick Adams transferred in for his senior year and would be counted on as a change-of-pace pass-receiving tight end to complement blocking tight end Galen Kellum. The skill players were extraordinary. No one doubted that the speed and talent of this group were championship caliber. Only one thing could derail the Purple Express.

"We did not know how our offensive line would gel. We didn't have as much experience as normal. Offensive line coach Steve Fentress did an amazing job helping mold the line."

Only one offensive position needed to be filled, the one W.T. considered the most important role on offense. Quarterback? Running back? Nope.

Center.

Johnston identified one player who could make a difference in that role. "I sat down with Avante Burnham and challenged him to move to that position. He was reluctant because he wanted to be a defensive player, and he could have been a great one there. But I told him the truth: 'If you play center like I believe you can, we will be state champions.'"

Avante and his dad agreed to sacrifice personal desires for the team. The first and most important O-line piece of the puzzle was in place. Right tackle Caiden Walker was an imposing figure at six foot five and 290 pounds. "Caiden and Avante are the most physical players on the line. Caiden has great feet, and I would have played him at tight end if we didn't need him at tackle."

Right guard Jamarion Samuel was promoted from the junior varsity squad and helped solidify the line. His persistent pleas to be moved up to varsity finally paid off. "We called him 'the Tick' because we couldn't get rid of him," W.T. says, chuckling. "He was relentless in the weight room and on the field, advancing his cause. We gave him a chance and he came through."

The left guard might have been only five foot nine, but teammates agreed that Patrick Davis was the strongest player on the team. He lined up alongside another guy who needed to believe in himself and what he meant to the success of the team. W.T. tapped William Steel for left tackle, a critical role for the Eagles and the focus of the 2009 movie *The Blind Side*. The left tackle protects the quarterback from his back or blind side and is crucial to offensive success. "I told William he needed to be that guy. Every championship team has a senior or two who step into the gap and make the difference. I challenged William to be one of those guys.

"You take twenty-two kids with twenty-two different personalities and stories and try every year to make them play as one. Our secret to success is not that complicated. You have a set of rules that is color-blind and unrelated to talent. The rules apply the same to the four-star recruit as they do to the last substitute in the game. You always tell the players the truth and, above all else, are fair to every single kid. You coach them hard and let them know you love them. It is a pretty simple formula that has worked pretty well."

Kristi Staley marvels at how W.T. leads his team. "He truly sees no race. They are just his kids, and W.T. strives to be a lasting influence. You have to understand that so many of these boys come from difficult backgrounds. The locker room is their home and their sanctuary. W.T. is the only father figure for many of them."

Perhaps you can control the message and method, but W.T. Johnston knew very well there are some things you can't control. The weather is one of them. Just as Hurricane Rita had in 2005, Mother Nature rearranged the upcoming football season. This time it was Hurricane Harvey that brought high winds and massive flooding. Newton County recorded fifty inches of rain, and the Sabine River couldn't be contained. The Houston area got most of the headlines from the storm, but Harvey hit southeastern Texas hard.

That only raised the expectations in Newton even more. You see, in 1998 a major fire burned down the elementary school. The Eagles won their first state crown. In 2005 the town was devasted by Hurricane Rita. State title number two. Now with another disaster wreaking havoc, the talk was that Newton was positioned for their third championship. W.T. believed in hard work and preparation more than omens, but he did note the coincidence.

This time school was only postponed for a week. Instead of preparing for their first game, the coaches were helping to rescue players and their families trapped by flooded roads. Practice resumed before school began, and the team was able to get back on the field after missing just one game.

The first game against the Silsbee Tigers looked like a challenge for the Eagles, coming off a week of nearly nonexistent practices. Silsbee brought an experienced and athletic squad to Singletary Stadium. Wide receiver Kalon Barnes was one of the fastest players in the country and held the Texas high school hundred-yard dash record.

The Newton team's timing was off early on, but it was clear that this group could be special, especially on the defensive side of the ball. Drew Johnston was impressed. "We were physical, and we knew then we were going to be really good on defense." The defense only gave up ten points to a talented team. Drew did point out to someone close to him how the other touchdown was scored.

"We gave up seven points because the head coach made a horrible judgment call," W.T. says, laughing. "I decided to punt away to the fastest kid in Texas with two minutes remaining in the half. He ran by me so fast on the sideline my hat spun around!" That return narrowed the halftime margin to three: 20–17.

Back on the field for the third quarter, the Newton offense showed how explosive they could be as Darwin Barlow plowed for more than two hundred yards and two touchdowns. The new starting quarterback Josh Foster added 88 yards on the ground and two more touchdowns while adding another 122 yards through the air. One of the players that Johnston and Coach Neece were counting on was senior wide receiver Noah Williams. With all-everything wide receiver Taumazia Brown lined up on the other side and getting lots of double team attention, Williams would get a chance to shine.

Tonight was not that night. W.T. recalls how much a difficult night affected Williams.

"Noah dropped four sure touchdown passes in the game. He was so despondent after the game that I was worried about him. I called him and texted him. I told him we were going to keep throwing him the ball. We had more confidence in him than he did in himself. He must have sat in front of his locker for two hours after the game."

The Eagles soared to a satisfying 41–17 win over a good team, but the most important takeaway from this game was making sure the very talented senior wide receiver did not lose his confidence. W.T. knew that how the staff and the talented Williams handled this night would be critical to the team's ultimate success. "By Monday we were joking with Noah and telling him we were throwing him the ball this week. It was his choice if he was going to catch it or get embarrassed."

Coach Blake Morrison brought his Diboll Lumberjacks to Newton the following week. Johnston describes his opponent with admiration. "Without a doubt, they were one of the best teams we would play all year. I think they were the most physical and featured the best offensive line we faced all season. Coach Morrison does a good job with his kids."

The Lumberjacks loaded up to slow down Darwin Barlow and had some success, as the junior could only muster seventy yards and one touchdown. The versatility of offensive coordinator Greg Neece's unit was apparent as Josh Foster lofted four touchdown passes in the game. Three scores went to Taumazia Brown, and Noah Williams snagged his first touchdown catch of the season. Diboll would eventually make it to the third round of the play-offs, and W.T. knew that a 40–20 win over this team was showing good progress.

Newton traveled to Bridge City for what was always a physical challenge. Darwin Barlow racked up 170 yards and three touchdowns. Josh Foster found Brown for two passing scores and Noah Williams for another. The Eagles left the Cardinals smarting from a 55–14 loss.

The first non–Mother Nature challenge for the team came the week before facing East Chambers. W.T.'s blood treatment at MD Anderson took precedence over football, and he couldn't be there for practice. Drew ran the team through drills that week, and the kids seemed to be handling everything okay. But they missed their head coach—every day they asked Drew if W.T. would be back for the game.

At first that looked like a possibility, but as the week progressed, it seemed less likely that Johnston would be on the sideline. One particular player was struggling with W.T.'s absence.

Darwin Barlow asked his mom, Michelle Gilder, if he could go see Johnston before the game. Gilder understood. Johnston had been her physical education teacher years ago. She understood the emotional connection of football in Newton, which she fondly calls "Friday night church."

"I just don't think I can play if I don't know how he is doing," Darwin told her. That strong bond Darwin had with W.T. had never wavered from the time he followed him around with the oxygen tank cart. It mattered much more to him than football. Gilder got her son excused on Thursday, and they drove four hours to Houston.

Just a few minutes away from the hospital, Darwin asked his mom to stop at a convenience store. She didn't think much of it. Maybe he needed a bathroom break or he wanted a drink. When Darwin got back in the car, he held up a big bag of Jolly Ranchers.

Darwin's unexpected visit surprised and touched W.T. It was somewhat unsettling for Darwin to see his source of strength sedated in a hospital bed. W.T. remembers Darwin's concern. "I was a bit drugged up, and I think Darwin thought I was worse than I actually was. But his concern meant a lot to me and showed me again how God was using me in the lives of these young men."

Four hours later, Barlow left more determined than ever. "I realized we had to get this title for him."

W.T. missed the game, but the team connected him via FaceTime to a television in the locker room. He gave the players reassuring talks before they took the field and later at halftime.

The East Chambers Buccaneers ran into a motivated team determined not to let their coach down. Without a doubt Darwin Barlow was able to play after seeing his coach. He tallied 180 yards and four touchdowns on only sixteen carries. The junior running back averaged a staggering eleven yards per carry, and the Eagles remained undefeated.

W.T. returned for the next district game against Crockett. The Bulldogs of Coach Jimmy Thompson were usually a team that caused concern, but the week leading up to the game had been devastating for them.

Crockett senior Tyress Anderson had died in a single-car crash the night after the school's homecoming game. The team, school, and community were reeling from the shocking loss.

"When Tyress walked into a room, the room became brighter," Coach Thompson said in tribute. "He was smiling, dancing, joking, and having a good time with his teammates."

Debbie Johnston remembers the atmosphere's being unlike anything she had witnessed in high school football. "It was somber and surreal. It was clear how much their kids were struggling with all this heartbreaking news."

Tyress Anderson's family asked W.T. if he would talk with them, and he was honored to comply. They represented their son at the coin toss and spent some private moments with W.T. before the game. W.T. was able to share his sympathy and prayed with the grieving family. Again, God was using his trials to help others.

The game seemed almost like an afterthought. The Eagles won handily on a night that was about more than winning and losing on the field.

The Garrison Bulldogs were next for Newton, arriving with some funky new formations and a good game plan. They slowed down the Eagles for a while, but the team eventually rolled to a 58–0 final for win number six.

The Eagles traveled twenty-five miles down Highway 59 the following Friday to meet the Corrigan-Camden Bulldogs. They left with their second consecutive shutout after tallying fifty-two points.

It was on the Hemphill sideline forty-three years ago that a young ball boy had seensaw up close and personal how good the Newton

Eagles were. Who knew he would be the man calling the shots for that team four decades later?

The location had changed but the results had not. Newton cruised to a 75–0 win over Hemphill for their eighth win of the year. Were these routs running up the score? "We do everything we can to keep the score down," W.T. explains. "Our star players often play just the first half. Darwin Barlow might have been able to set a yardage record, but he was pulled out after two quarters. Sometimes we kick a field goal instead of trying to score a touchdown. But I can't ask our younger players not to try."

Linebacker Corbin Foster good-naturedly accused the coaches of collusion when he came out of a game early. Foster was chasing the all-time single season record for tackles, a record that was held by defensive coordinator Drew Johnston. "Corbin always got mad when I would pull him out," Drew says, laughing. "But he got my record and he deserved it." Corbin finished the year with 232 tackles to eclipse his coach's previous mark of 204.

Providing extra playing time for the lesser-known players pays big dividends for the Newton program. "Our backups get lots of playing time," W.T. reflects. "When someone gets hurt, they are able to step in and lean on that experience. And when players graduate, their backups always have had time on the field."

The Eagles finished district play with a win over the Frankston Indians 47–0. Coach Drew Johnston's defense had posted three straight shutouts to finish an undefeated regular season.

For Newton fans, the preseason was over. The regular season—the play-offs—would begin the following week against the team that had crushed their hopes the year before.

18

LORD, LET ME FINISH THIS

W.T. Johnston did not know how much longer he would be able to coach. The experimental treatments had kept the GvHD symptoms at bay. As far as most people knew, Johnston had dodged that bullet, and he was as healthy as he had been for a while. What they didn't know was that doctors were not able to prevent his body from rejecting the new lungs. W.T. was slowly losing lung capacity, and doctors felt his body could not handle the rigors of a second lung transplant.

Most smart people were not about to wager against W.T. Johnston's beating the odds. The average life span of a patient diagnosed with GvHD was 280 days. Johnston was approaching the nine hundredth sunrise since his diagnosis day. The doctors at MD Anderson were writing articles for medical journals about the unassuming football coach from small-town Texas. Calls came in from around the world to MD Anderson requesting the clinical reports so others could find out how W.T. had managed to triple his expected survival time.

W.T. knew a lot of factors played into his still being around. So many people in Newton, Texas, and around the world were praying. "There is a song by Ricky Skaggs called 'Somebody's Prayin'.' In the lyrics he describes how 'I can feel it' when people are praying. I completely understand that. Debbie and I could feel the prayers for us. Without a doubt."

Another factor was the group of kids he coached. "This group is not the most talented we have ever had at Newton. In 2001 we had four players that I thought could have played on Sundays in the NFL, and that team did not win the title. This group was a team. It is the loosest and the most inclusive team I have ever been around."

Juraj Kolenic experienced firsthand how welcoming this community is when he arrived as a foreign exchange student from Slovakia.

Newton doesn't have a soccer team. Eric and Missy Dunn were the host family for Kolenic. They introduced him to W.T. to see if he could be a placekicker for the Eagles.

"He didn't know how to kick a football. Some of the players showed him how to tee it up and kick. I went out to the field to audition him, thinking that maybe he could help as a manager or something. After two kicks I was scrambling for the paperwork to get him eligible. He had a strong leg. We had a capable kicker in Caleb Colon, but now we had a backup and a kicker for long field goal tries if that came up. Juraj had more than enough leg to make it from forty-five yards out."

The team immediately embraced Juraj, but they did make one small adjustment. They had a hard time pronouncing his name, so they changed it. Drawing inspiration from the movie *The Waterboy* about a walk-on player with unexpected talent who had a hard-kicking mule named Steve, they landed on a new moniker for Juraj. Imagine him trying to explain that to the folks back in Slovakia.

"My teammates call me Steve because ... never mind. They just call me Steve."

Thinking about Juraj always brings a smile to W.T.'s face. "The kids loved him. He would sit with the black kids at lunch. It showed the acceptance of this team."

The kids made W.T. laugh, and they gave him a reason to get going in the morning, especially during this tough season. "No one knew that I punctured a lung before the first game. The doctors told me it might have come from yelling at a player. I am pretty sure it was Darwin Barlow I was yelling at."

Doctors again wanted W.T. to take a break from the sideline. "They wanted to put me in the hospital, but I said no. I just fought through it and the puncture healed. I was not going to miss time with this group if I could help it. I had missed enough already."

This team was the healing energy that got W.T. through the increasing pain of each day. The moments he got to spend inside the white lines reinforced his always upbeat response to anyone who expressed sympathy.

"I have been given a great gift to see how my life matters."

Now Coach Johnston was asking for another gift of time. He wanted to see this special group of young men and coaches through the play-off process. Without question he wanted to have a ring for himself. Every high school football coach in Texas desired that. Even more, he wanted it for these kids who loved him and motivated him to fight through his excruciating daily pain. He wanted it for Coach Neece, who had made personal and career sacrifices to be a part of this quest. He wanted it for Newton, a community that found so much joy and significance through their Purple Pride. W.T. wanted it for Debbie. No one knew how much she had endured and how much strength she had provided to make this dream possible. He wanted it for Shaw. His youngest son had flirted with coaching. Both Coach Barbay and W.T. had taught him that you are a teacher first and a coach second. It was something Shaw thought through carefully.

"I could have happily coached football for the rest of my life, but I knew I was not passionate about teaching. It wasn't fair to the kids if I didn't have that drive to teach, so I decided to pursue another direction." Shaw had fashioned a successful career in Houston representing an industrial supply and foundry company. But he knew the pressure of this moment and felt it for his dad and brother.

W.T. wanted it for Drew. W.T. could see how much pressure his oldest son was putting on himself to secure a title for his dad. He couldn't help but notice an uncharacteristic edge to Drew when things were not going well in practice and games. W.T. and Debbie were truly concerned about how their son would cope if the team fell short again. But W.T. knew that Drew would have to work this out himself, and he chose not to call attention to it.

All of this provided the backdrop to W.T.'s simple prayer entering the 2017 University Interscholastic League (UIL) football play-offs.

"Lord, let me live long enough to see this through."

19

THE SECOND SEASON

For Newton Eagles fans, the regular season is a nice little Friday night diversion until the play-offs begin. Now it was about to get real, and W.T. Johnston thrived on the expectations.

"Not everyone can play on this big stage. Lidney Thompson and Curtis Barbay set the bar high. I love the challenge and so do the kids. They expect to be playing in the final game every year."

The play-offs opened with a revenge match. The Arp Tigers had spoiled last year's play-off run, and they had the unenviable task of being Newton's first opponent.

"We don't talk about revenge, but the kids were well aware of who they were playing."

Especially Arp's star player, high school all-American and Texas Longhorns recruit DeMarvion Overshown. Talk about additional motivation!

"Our kids love going against the best. They were begging me to have us kick to DeMarvion so they could have a chance to tackle him."

Arp was not going to be the spoiler again. Newton cruised to a 58–0 win behind six touchdowns from Darwin Barlow. Drew Johnston's Seven Diamond had now gone twenty-one quarters without giving up a touchdown.

The next opponent, the Rice Bulldogs, was located about forty-five minutes south of Dallas in Navarro County. Since it was a hefty three-hundred-mile drive between the two schools, Crockett, Texas, was picked as a logical midpoint location for the game. One of the challenges of the long play-off slate is playing during the holidays. The Thanksgiving week game meant preparing both turkey and game plans. W.T. did not think the latter was going all that well. "We did not have a good week of practice, and that is a little scary in the play-offs. The kids knew they should win, and that is a little scary, too, when you combine those two factors and the loser goes home till next year."

Newton was sloppy but simply had too much firepower for the Bulldogs. Rice was able to break the shutout streak, but the Eagles prevailed 65–11.

Round three can be a trap week for teams that let down their guard. "At this point anybody can beat you if you don't play. We were facing a team on the rise, and they were fired up for a shot at the top seed."

The West Rusk Raiders were indeed on a roll. Their only loss had been a heart-stopping one-point defeat to Elysian Fields, and after that Coach John Frazier's team had reeled off four straight convincing wins.

"They knew how much support the community gives our team, so West Rusk was determined not to play too close to Newton. In Texas the UIL coordinates the state tournament and play-off locations. When coaches can't agree on a neutral site, they sometimes resort to creative solutions," W.T. explains.

"We met with their coaches and a representative of the UIL at a Whataburger in Marshall and flipped a coin to determine where we would play. They won the flip, but at least I got a good burger out of the trip."

Coach Frazier chose Tatum as the game site. "I didn't blame him," W.T. reflects. "He was trying to give his kids every chance, and Tatum was only thirty minutes away from their fans in New London. We had to travel over two hours to get to the game."

Still, no one was surprised that the stands were awash with purple when the ball was kicked off. "We knew this might be our biggest challenge. At that point, the Raiders had a kid committed to Texas A&M. We felt like this was our big hurdle to get back to the championship."

Tyree Wilson was impressive at six foot six, an intimidating defensive presence for the opponents. "West Rusk was the best defensive team we played all year. They had a lot of good athletes, and Coach Frazier had a good plan."

Newton fans might have had bad flashbacks to the Arp game when the Raiders scored on their second offensive play to knot the score at seven apiece. Darwin Barlow ran for a touchdown to put Newton up by seven. Josh Foster tallied the only second-quarter points for Newton with a rushing score.

The Eagle defense only gave up seventy-four total yards, but turnovers gave West Rusk chances to score. "We gave up an interception in the red zone, and they got the ball to the five-yard line with a first down. Our defense held."

Johnston knows how any play-off run has a play that turns the tide. That play came in the third quarter with the game still in doubt. The Eagles faced a daunting third and twenty-two play from their own thirty. "Kevin Watson came in, we ran the trap, and he got twenty-two and a half. That was the play of the game."

Darwin Barlow was critical in Newton's control of the clock, especially down the stretch when Newton was determined to keep the ball away from the Raiders.

Newton escaped with a hard-fought 21–7 victory. W.T. knew this would likely be the team's biggest test until they reached AT&T Stadium. "We hadn't had to struggle in any games that year," Johnston says. "This was going to help us down the road. I was wondering if we got in a game like this what we would do. Our defense stood up. It was unbelievable." He also had high praise for his former "oxygen buddy," Darwin Barlow. "Darwin is a special kid. People don't realize he is only sixteen. His best football is still ahead of him."

On paper, Johnston had suspected that West Rusk was the team with the best shot to ground the Eagles, but every game going forward would require focused effort. Waskom, the same school that handed Newton a crushing defeat in the 2014 championship, was the next opponent.

Blowing sleet and snow flurries greeted the team and fans on December 8 as they entered Abe Martin Stadium in Lufkin. Newton fans were bundled up but still shivered in freezing temperatures as they awaited the 7:30 kickoff. They only had to wait eleven seconds for Darwin Barlow to break off a sixty-nine-yard touchdown sprint on the first offensive play. The injury-depleted Wildcats could not stop the Eagles, and the halftime score was 35–6. The Newton coaches got the rare opportunity to get some play-off rest for their starters in the second half of the game on their way to a 45–6 final. One game remained before W.T. Johnston could return to Arlington for the big game.

The Boling Bulldogs had made it to the state title game in 2016 and were looking to return. Boling had also lost some early-season games to Hurricane Harvey and started off slowly. Behind Alabama commit Vernon Jackson, the team had reeled off four straight wins, and they were playing their best football of the season heading into the semifinal game with Newton. Jackson was a big-time talent who would later switch his commitment from the Tide to enroll at Texas A&M. The game would be played in Porter, Texas, just north of Houston.

"Coach Kevin Urbanek had a great scheme. They moved Jackson from quarterback to running back and lined him up eight yards deep. The offensive line lined up foot to foot with no gaps for the defenders to shoot. It was like a rugby scrum with this 240-pound battering ram hitting our defense."

Vernon Jackson led the team down the field for an early score. Newton fumbled the ensuing kickoff, and Jackson ran it for another score. Newton trailed by fourteen in the first quarter.

"There was no panic, but the kids were concerned. The coaches were wondering if we could stop Jackson. Once we had him dead to rights for a safety, and he threw off a couple of tacklers and ran thirty yards."

When you are down, you find out what you are made of. Coach Greg Neece went to a hurry-up offense, and the Eagles got their first touchdown. A forced Boling turnover led to another score; Newton had fought back to even things up after one quarter.

Boling responded with a touchdown to go up 21–14. Newton was in a nerve-racking battle in their quest to return to the state championship game.

On the Eagles' next possession, they faced a third and seventeen. Coach Neece had an ace up his sleeve, and now was the time to play that card. The team had been practicing a play all season to use when they needed a lift. The "hook and lateral" play started with a quick hook pattern to Noah Williams and an immediate lateral to a streaking Darwin Barlow. Seventy yards later, Barlow found pay dirt, and the game was again tied at twenty-one. Newton scored two more times before halftime and took a twelve-point lead into the locker room.

This was a heavyweight matchup with the winner fighting for a shot at the crown.

Boling's strategy was to keep pounding the Newton defense with punishing runs from Jackson. The Bulldogs passed the ball just one time in the contest for only four yards. In the second half, Boling drove for a touchdown to pull to within six points. This one was far from over.

There was something special about this group and their desire to get to the final game. Boling drove deep into Newton territory with a chance to regain the lead. It was time for the defense to rise up. The Eagles stuffed Boling on fourth down, and their own star running back went to work.

Darwin Barlow broke off long touchdown runs of forty-seven and sixty-three yards. "I knew we needed that extra push late in the game to get the win," Barlow says. "I just wanted to do anything I could to get us to the championship game, and I think I did that with those two touchdowns."

Newton scored twenty-three unanswered points. With each series, the defense became more confident as the workload began to wear down talented Bulldog running back Vernon Jackson. The final score, 56–28, did not reflect how tough this game had been. Boling had given the Newton Eagles their best shot, and the team weathered the blow.

A relieved W.T. Johnston said Vernon Jackson was the best player his team had faced during the season. "He's a special talent," Johnston said. "We hadn't faced anyone who could do the kind of things he did out there. He might be the best player we've ever faced."

Jackson would finish the night with 235 yards on forty-three punishing carries against one of the best defenses in the state.

The Eagles had landed in the final game. "I wasn't always sure about this team earlier in the year, but I was sure now," he said. "This team didn't think anyone could beat them, and they might have been right."

Coach Johnston's health was an ongoing concern. "My prayer was simple. 'Give me one more week. I want to finish this journey with these special kids.'"

20

CHAMPIONSHIP WEEK

They had made it to the last game. Both W.T. and Drew knew from painful personal experience how much it hurt to lose a final game. Drew was more determined to make sure that didn't happen than he had ever been about anything.

The opponent was daunting. The Gunter Tigers were bringing a thirty-one-game winning streak to Arlington. They featured a staunch defense and talented offensive. Gunter had the advantage of a much shorter road trip to AT&T Stadium. The town is situated only sixty miles northeast of Arlington. The Newton fans would have the longer drive, with a nearly five-hour trek to cheer their team.

The Tigers were the defending state champions after demolishing Boling 43–7 in the final game of 2016. To say the Gunter fans were confident was an understatement.

Coach Johnston may be old school, but he is aware of the impact of social media. "Some of their fans posted negative things about Newton. They made comments about how the disciplined kids from their school would handle the undisciplined athletes from Newton. I made sure we printed out some of those observations for our players to see." W.T. smiles as he finishes the story. "They didn't really appreciate the stereotype."

Drew Johnston knew that was a dangerous assumption. "Our kids don't have a lot. We live in a world of haves and have-nots. Our kids were hungry to show they belonged in that world. Add in the motivation to win for my dad, and you had a pretty dangerous team to face."

The demands of championship week were draining for W.T. His lung capacity was diminishing at an alarming rate, and he tried not to think about the possibilities. He was not going to wear oxygen on the sideline—by the grace of God. One more week was all he asked God to grant him.

And what a week this would be. W.T. had learned a lot in that first championship game. "That first state title game was a blur. We weren't prepared like we are used to being prepared. We traveled the day of the game, and that was a mistake. This time I took all day Saturday after the Boling game to put the itinerary together. We set up to travel the day before and stay in Ennis, about fifty miles away. Then we could practice at Ennis High School's facility courtesy of my friend Jack Alvarez."

Another lesson learned was how to navigate the weird schedule of the UIL championship tournament. Teams are only allowed to come into the facility at prescribed times. In 2014 the team went straight to their locker room, and the first time they saw the field was during pregame warm-ups. "This year we got to watch the game before us and get used to the atmosphere. That was huge for us. For small-town kids, it was like a scene from the movie *Hoosiers* where the coach shows them that the court is just like the one back home in Hickory, Indiana. Our kids could see that even with the giant scoreboard and a hundred thousand seats, the field was still a hundred yards long and fifty-three yards wide. Just like in Newton. All we needed to do was concentrate on what happened between those white lines."

Johnston felt good as he reviewed the videos of his opponent. They were clearly a good team, but so were the Eagles. "Everybody was talking about Gunter. I think they forgot that we were pretty good too."

21

CHAMPIONSHIP DAY

W.T. Johnston sat alone in a service tunnel inside the cavernous home of the Dallas Cowboys. From his folding chair, he could hear the cacophony of sounds as two high schools—Brock and Rockdale—battled for a state title. Soon he would lead his Newton Eagles football team against undefeated Gunter for the UIL 3A Division II Championship of Texas. Johnston's mind raced as he considered the miracle of this moment. Most Texas high school coaches only dreamed of being on this stage.

He chuckled to himself. The entire population of Newton would fit forty times into AT&T Stadium with just a few seats left over. He knew that most of the town had made the 265-mile trek from Newton County to Texas football's crown-jewel facility.

Three years earlier, Johnston had had his first chance as a head coach to win a title on this very field. The dream ended in a disappointing loss to Waskom High School. On this FridayThursday in December, he would try again to win an elusive state title against the defending state champ that sported a daunting thirty-one-game winning streak. Most experts picked the Gunter Tigers to repeat as champs. That didn't bother Johnston too much, since most experts expected him to be dead.

He had been praying for God to allow him to live long enough to see this moment, and now it was here. It was almost certain this would be his last chance for a head coach championship ring in only his eighth season at the helm.

Not many people outside Newton knew his story. Most of the crowd cheering their high school teams here in Arlington had no idea what Coach Johnston had endured to make it to this moment. Almost no one knew that he had collapsed earlier in the day, not even his son Drew. The coaches who had witnessed that scary incident worried that it could happen again, and maybe the results would be worse.

Johnston pondered what this game meant. He knew he would be okay personally if the results weren't good. Sure, it would be a disappointment because it is never fun to lose that final game. But the folks in Newton? This would mean so much to a town that had endured more than its share of adversity.

He thought about his family. Son Drew was his defensive coordinator who had previously won a 2005 state title as a Newton Eagle player when W.T. was Coach Barbay's assistant. The family didn't discuss the real chance that this could be W.T.'s final shot. He wanted this for Debbie, Drew, and Shaw more than he did for himself.

He thought about those sixty kids who would soon take the field— the same field that Ezekiel Elliott, Tony Romo, and Jason Witten had excelled on. Standing for the coin flip on that famous Cowboy star that measures ten yards from point to point. Trying to avoid staring at the ridiculously huge video screen that verifies outsiders' notions that everything is bigger in Texas.

W.T. knew how much the players wanted to win it for him, but he wanted it even more for them. He knew that long after he was gone, this moment would be something special for these young men. Most of the kids were poor, and this was an experience that they would treasure forever. W.T. wanted them to finish their high school football careers with a state championship ring.

Television announcer Ron Thulin approached W.T. and sat with him for a few minutes. Thulin would be doing the play-by-play on Fox Sports Southwest that day. He remarked how W.T.'s response to adversity had inspired him.

W.T. looked at Thulin and smiled. "Ron, most people don't have a chance to really see how their lives have mattered. They don't get the perspective to treasure each day. I have been given a great gift."

As Thulin headed to the broadcast booth, Johnston took one more moment to remember the gift of life and the gift of this moment. No matter what happened in the next four hours, he believed this promise from the Bible:

Those who trust in the LORD will find new strength.
They will soar high on wings like eagles.
They will run and not grow weary.
They will walk and not faint.
Isaiah 40:31, NLT

22

THE BIG STAGE

It is almost impossible to comprehend what it is like for a sixteen-year-old boy to run onto the Dallas Cowboys' home field to play for a state championship. Kids who have played in front of a few dozen or a few hundred look at a vast sea of faces. They struggle to balance fear and exhilaration. Some teams thrive on this big stage, and others wilt. The Newton Eagles always looked to one source of strength in these moments: their coach.

"There is nothing like being in the battle with these young men," W.T. says. "One of the things I love the most about coaching is the team huddle. It is a sacred place that only I get to share with my players. No one else gets to invade that sacred space between the white lines. I always ask them to take a knee, and I get down to their level. I look in their eyes, and I see what is going on in their hearts and minds. Sometimes I see fear. Sometimes I see anger. Sometimes I see confidence.

W.T. huddles with his team.
(Courtesy Newtonsports.com/
Sherry Tracy)

Sometimes I see overconfidence. When I look in their eyes, I know what I need to say in that moment. I will miss that more than anything when I am done coaching."

On this Thursday, December 21, 2017, Coach Johnston saw a team that was ready. A team that wanted to win for their coach and their community. His job today would be to keep them from getting too emotionally charged up and to focus only on the task at hand. Johnston knew they had a good plan. But when you deal with high school boys, you never know exactly what will happen.

The Newton community had shown up in all their purple splendor. There was no school on Thursday and Friday. Newton looked like a ghost town on Thursday afternoon, as everyone who could take time off hit Highway 190 to Arlington. Those who had to remain behind were glued to the broadcast of the game. Many gathered to watch on a big screen at a somewhat unlikely location—the Son Asian Bistro in Jasper. Championship day in Newton rivaled Christmas Day in anticipation and excitement.

The Newton cheerleaders were wide-eyed as they walked onto the field. The Eagle mascot ran along the sideline where Dallas Cowboy mascot Rowdy would be pumping up a hundred thousand hometown fans in just two days.

It was a surreal and magical atmosphere. The tension in the stands was palpable for the Newton fans and particularly Debbie Johnston. "You always want to win, but the stakes for this game were so much higher. I knew that short of a miracle, this would be W.T.'s last chance. I was a nervous wreck."

As in every other time in their relationship, she knew her husband was calm. "His strength in these moments is my rock, and he is the rock for the team as well."

The teams finished their warm-ups and went to the locker room for the final moments before kickoff.

W.T. called his team around him.

"Everybody thinks Gunter is the smart and disciplined team. The experts keep saying how good they are. But the experts are forgetting something that everyone in this room knows. We are pretty darn good too."

The team knelt together as W.T. Johnston prayed before the Eagles took the field. They were ready to leave it all on the field for their God, town, school, coach, and teammates.

With an earsplitting roar, the team ran into that magnificent venue with their coach trailing behind. W.T. tried to savor the moment. This was what coaching was all about—hard work, teamwork, grinding, and mental toughness. Months of early-morning workouts in a spartan facility that would be laughed at by the big school programs. Boys becoming men in the pressure of lofty expectations. Living life in a locker room with young men and teaching them about football and life. This was what God put W.T. Johnston on this planet to do, and he was more than grateful for this moment. And if the outcome was a championship, well, that was a bonus.

W.T. walked to the sideline, the place that gave him such joy. "Between the white lines is the purest and most real place you can be. There is no black or white. No rich or poor. No conservative or liberal. It is just competition."

He had taught his players that there was another dimension inside those white lines where it was only one another.

"I taught them to find Christ inside those white lines. Jesus epitomizes the equal playing field. Paul wrote there is no Jew or Gentile. No free man or slave. We are all the same inside those theological white lines. Don't ever let anyone tell you that you don't matter. You do."

Johnston stopped to breathe a prayer. The moment was here. He looked up as Gunter placekicker Evan Gonzalez launched the opening kickoff. God had answered his prayer. He was here with his team. He had been given a great gift.

23

FIRST QUARTER

This matchup of two great teams was like a heavyweight championship boxing match. The first few punches and jabs are getting a rhythm and trying to find weaknesses. Josh Foster led the Eagles on the first drive of the game. Darwin Barlow scampered for a first down on the first set of downs. Two incomplete passes followed by a four-yard quarterback keeper forced Newton to punt.

Gunter gained nine yards on their first two running plays and faced a third and one. The Newton defense stuffed Braiden Clopton on a great defensive surge led by Dominique Seastrunk. The first round of downs was a draw, and it looked as if this could be a defensive battle.

The Eagles' second offense series never really got off the ground. Gage Biggerstaff stopped Darwin Barlow for a loss. A motion penalty on the offensive line set them back five more yards. A short run and an incompletion forced Newton into another punting situation.

"We started a little shaky. That is not surprising in this game on this stage," Johnston recalls. "Our punt team was not used to working that much in the first quarter."

Gunter had good field position on their own forty-two-yard line as they began their second set of downs. A couple of running plays set up

BETWEEN THE WHITE LINES

a manageable third and three play. Newton linebacker Corbin Foster sniffed out the play and tackled quarterback Daylan Bower for a loss. The Tigers trotted out their punt team for a second time, and a good punt pinned Newton inside the ten-yard line.

The Newton fans were growing a little anxious. The defense was playing as they had hoped, but so far the explosive offense had not arrived.

Another motion penalty on the offense gave Coach Neece's offense a first and fifteen start. Josh Foster ran a quarterback keeper for eight yards to give them some breathing room. But two more runs left the Eagles two yards short, and they punted for the third time. The field position game was favoring Gunter as they took over on their own forty-two-yard line with a new set of downs.

Gunter's first two plays netted just a yard and forced the Tigers to go to the air. Newton was ready. Coach Drew Johnston dialed up some pressure. Linebacker Jadrian McGraw forced Bower to throw on the run and into the waiting arms of Newton defensive back Taumazia Brown at the Eagles' twenty-eight-yard line. The elusive Brown wove forty-four yards to the Gunter twenty-eight. The purple cheering section came to life. On the first play after the turnover, Coach Neece called a fake reverse to Brown with Darwin Barlow keeping the handoff instead. Gunter went with the misdirection, and Barlow streaked down the right sideline, juked a defender at the five-yard line, and crossed the goal line for the first score of the game. Caleb Colon's extra point try split the uprights, and Newton led 7–0.

After the kick return, the Tigers went back on offense at their own thirty-nine-yard line. On the second play, Dylan Jantz broke off a thirty-three-yard run, and the Gunter fans got loud. Facing a third and ten, the Tigers dialed up a run by Braiden Clopton that just netted enough for a first down at the thirteen.

Gunter ground out another first down to the three-yard line before Peyton Lowe ran untouched for a score. Kicker Evan Gonzalez converted the extra point to tie the score at seven.

The kickoff put the ball at the twenty-five, and another motion penalty set the chains at first and fifteen. Darwin Barlow broke off a long gainer on second down all the way to the Gunter forty-eight. A short two-yard run ended the first quarter with the powerhouse programs even at seven. This game was delivering on all the hype.

24

SECOND QUARTER

Except for one big play, the normally spectacular Eagle offense had been quiet. Uncharacteristic penalties had put them in difficult situations. Part of that was getting used to the weird vibe of indoor football in this gigantic venue. The blaring public address speakers, the supersized video screen, and the massive structure itself were distracting. But W.T. knew his players needed to sharpen up to win this game.

Positive running plays by Kevin Watson Jr., Darwin Barlow, and Josh Foster and a big gainer by Taumazia Brown placed the ball at the Gunter eleven-yard line.

On the next play, Foster dropped and lofted a beautiful fade pass to a leaping Noah Williams. The angular wide receiver pulled it down, and the Eagles regained the lead. The successful kick made it a 14–7 tally with nine minutes left in the half.

Gunter started at their own twenty-nine, and Peyton Lowe quickly ripped off a thirteen-yard gain for a first down. Two plays later, Braiden Clopton raced all the way to the Newton twenty-five, and the momentum shifted again. Another first down put the ball at the fifteen. The Eagles called a time-out as Drew Johnston exhorted his defenders. It was time for someone to "rise up" and make a play. That player was linebacker

Jadrian McGraw, who blitzed and dropped Daylan Bower for a three-yard loss. The Eagles held on two more plays, and Gunter settled for a thirty-three-yard field goal from Evan Gonzalez to make it a 14–10 Newton lead.

After the kick, the Newton team again found themselves with poor field position as they started from the eleven. The Eagles managed one first down, but the offense sputtered and was forced to punt for the fourth time in the contest.

Gunter had a three and out possession and returned the ball on a punt. The Eagles had possession on their own forty with two minutes to go in this championship slugfest.

A forty-six-yard completion to Noah Williams put the Eagles in position to add to their lead. An apparent touchdown pass to Williams was called back for offensive pass interference. Two more false starts put the Newton offense in an impossible fourth and thirty-one with sixteen seconds left. Punt number five pinned the Tigers inside the ten with seconds left on the clock. Gunter decided to take a knee and get ready for the final half. It was the first time the Tigers had trailed halfway through the game all year.

W.T. Johnston was intercepted by reporter Sarah Merrifield on his way off the field. "We left too many points on the field. We have got to stop the penalties. We should be ahead by three touchdowns." His expression as he marched to the locker room suggested he might have to administer a little tough love inside. W.T. remembers that the halftime talk was a little more animated than usual. "We didn't make any defensive changes. Our base defense was working just fine. I had a little more to say to the offensive line. In fact, I might have chewed on our offensive line a little bit."

Offensive coordinator Greg Neece had seen some tendencies from the Gunter defense, so at halftime he drew up three plays that he hoped would counter the Gunter strategy.

The first play was a two tight end look with a fake reverse to Taumazia Brown. Noah Williams would run a snake route, and Josh Foster would throw to him. The second play would be a fake trap; Josh would stand up and throw to tight end Lakendrick Adams over the middle. The third play they diagrammed was a jet sweep to Taumazia Brown.

The penalties and missed plays were not the way Newton had gotten to this game. W.T. Johnston had made his point clear to his kids. In twenty-four minutes, the verdict would be in.

25

THIRD QUARTER

Gunter received the second-half kick and started from the twenty-seven-yard line. In the first half, Gunter had only managed twenty-eight yards of offense, all of that on the ground. Newton had sparkled on defense yet only held a four-point lead.

Gunter again went to the ground, and Newton held. The first series resulted in another punt to the Eagles. Then Newton gave Gunter just the gift they needed to regain momentum. A fumble gave the Tigers possession deep in Eagle territory. Quarterback Daylan Bower found a wide-open Braiden Clopton over the top for a twenty-three-yard score. A penalty on the first extra point try pushed the ball back. The second try was no good, as the ball banged off the uprights. Gunter had regained the lead 16–14 with a little more than eight minutes remaining in the third quarter.

Newton began their next series from the nineteen. Darwin Barlow immediately ripped off ten yards for a first down. Back-to-back runs by Foster and Brown advanced the ball to their forty-four. A long connection from Josh Foster to Noah Williams put Newton back into Gunter territory at the thirty-eight.

Again Darwin Barlow and Taumazia Brown ate up yardage on the ground, and Newton was in the red zone just fourteen yards away. This time the usually unflappable Josh Foster underthrew Noah Williams in the end zone, and two-way Gunter star Braiden Clopton intercepted and returned the ball to the Newton thirty-three.

It was gut check time again for Drew Johnston's Seven Diamond defense. Another Gunter score would increase the pressure on an offense that was struggling a bit.

Gunter got a third down conversion at their own forty-six, but star running back/receiver Dylan Jantz had to be helped off the field, and anxious Gunter fans feared that could be a big factor going forward. A holding penalty negated a nice gain and put the Tigers in a hole they could not escape. The good news for Gunter fans was that Dylan Jantz returned during the series. Gunter punted the ball back to Newton with just a couple of minutes left in the third quarter.

Starting at the nineteen, Newton went back to their strength. Three strong runs by Barlow moved the football to the forty-four-yard line. Coach Neece noticed that the Gunter defense was selling out more and more to stop the run by moving defenders up. They called play number one from the halftime adjustments. The defense bit on an apparent slot reverse to Taumazia Brown as Noah Williams slipped behind the pursuing secondary and was wide open. Gunter was able to put some pressure on Josh Foster, but he led Williams with a perfect pass. Williams pulled it in confidently and strolled into the end zone for a sixty-six-yard strike.

Remember that name? Noah Williams was the despondent wide receiver who dropped four sure touchdowns in the opening game of the season. The coaches believed in him and continued to have Foster throw to him. Now, on the biggest stage of his life, the senior receiver had two touchdown catches. W.T. Johnston and Greg Neece's belief in Williams's talent had restored the athlete's confidence, and now he was making a difference. Newton missed the point after, but as the third-quarter horn sounded, the Eagles held on to a perilous 20–16 lead. Twelve more minutes to heartbreak or happiness.

26

FOURTH QUARTER

The Newton defense was playing lights out. Three running plays resulted in no gain, a loss, and no gain. Gunter had to punt again. With nine minutes left in the game, it seemed like a logical time to go to the very effective running game of Barlow, Foster, Watson, and Brown. Running time off the clock would only help the Newton defense catch their breath and prepare to finish the task. Newton plays fewer two-way starters than most small schools. Only a handful on the roster went both ways, so Drew Johnston got to talk with most of his starters when the offense took the field.

One of W.T.'s core philosophies was about to come into play. "You can't just build up and count on your star players. You develop every kid and help him believe he will be ready when his moment comes. State titles are won when one or two unexpected players step up in a big way."

Gunter knew they had to stop the Eagles. Possessions were getting scarce. They were ready for Barlow, Foster, Brown, and Williams. Coach Neece called play number two from the halftime talks. Gunter did not focus enough on a slight tight end lined up on the right side. Senior Lakendrick Adams found an opening and hauled in a pass over the middle from Josh Foster. He split two surprised defenders and was off to the races for a seventy-five-yard score.

Again, the coaches' confidence in their players showed up. Foster had thrown an ugly interception early. Coaches Johnston and Neece knew that Josh had a short memory. They were not afraid to dial up a pass even if conventional wisdom said to run. Lakendrick Adams had been having a tough go in practice. But the coaches told him at halftime that they trusted him and he should be ready. He was. The extra point gave Newton a 27–16 advantage, but there was still more than nine minutes to go.

Gunter took over but still could not get untracked. A fumble was recovered by the offense, but it put the Tigers in a long third down situation. A pass completion came up well short. Gunter head coach Jeffrey Smith had to make a tough decision. It was fourth and twelve, deep in their own territory. The way the Newton offense was playing, they could not afford to give them the ball that close to the red zone. Gunter decided to punt once more.

Newton fans were beginning to breathe a little easier. Still, they knew a crucial turnover could swing the game back toward the Tigers quickly. They needed a good old grind-it-out Newton Eagle drive to eat into the last seven minutes.

Coach Neece and Taumazia Brown had other ideas—time to dial up play number three. Brown ran a jet sweep from Josh Foster and turned on the jets. The worn-down Gunter defense pursued the speedy wideout, but there was no catching Brown when he got the edge. Brown didn't take much time off the clock, but he did put up six points after a seventy-five-yard jaunt. The point after increased the Newton lead 34–16.

"It is pretty rare to draw up three plays and score on all three," Neece notes. "Maybe it was just meant to be for W.T." With the way the defense was playing, it looked as if the first title for W.T. Johnston was in sight.

Gunter was now forced to go to the air. Drew Johnston doesn't know how to spell *prevent defense*. He brought the house and made it difficult for quarterback Daylan Bower to find open receivers. Some hope remained for the defending state champs, until senior Newton defensive back Davien Johnson picked off a pass at midfield to seal the deal.

This time Newton would keep the ball on the ground, and the drive culminated with quarterback Josh Foster dancing eight yards into the end zone. The Newton Eagles had dropped forty points on a very good Gunter defense, recording a convincing 40–17 final. Perhaps more impressive was the amazing work on the defensive side of the ball. Against a powerful running team averaging 275 yards per game on the ground, the Eagles gave up only 137 on forty-four attempts. Coming into the final game, the Tigers were averaging fifty-six points a game in the play-offs, and they matched that number against an excellent squad from Canadian, Texas. The most points they had given up all year was twenty-seven. What Newton accomplished on this night against an undefeated defending state champ was indeed noteworthy.

As the final seconds ticked off the clock, the cameras caught an emotional Newton sideline. W.T. Johnston accepted hugs from coaches and players. When the final horn sounded, he dropped on all fours. Those nearby and watching on television held their breath. Was Coach okay? Later Johnston would laugh about what happened.

"I was praying and thanking God for that moment, and

W.T. Johnston is overcome with emotion at end of the State Title game.
(Courtesy Fox Sports Southwest)

nobody would leave me alone! They kept trying to help me up, and I was waving them off, trying to pray."

When he did stand up, one of the most poignant moments came when Drew embraced his dad with a hug. He acknowledged the weight and edginess he had been carrying with a trembling voice.

"I'm sorry. I wanted it so much for you."

W.T. held his son in a long embrace and simply said, "I know."

W.T. and Drew share an emotional moment.
(Courtesy Fox Sports Southwest)

Debbie and Shaw came down and joined the family embrace.

"I felt relief and pride," Shaw remembers. "My dad had sacrificed so much for us. We knew he had head coaching offers over the years, but he chose to stay for us to be a part of the Newton family. Drew got his championship in 2005. I fell just short in the title game in 2008. I was so grateful that Dad got this one."

Sideline reporter Sarah Merrifield caught up with Johnston for his postgame thoughts.

"Nobody is promised another day. Every day is special, and this is a real special one. I'm real proud of these kids, but I wanted to win this for the community of Newton. Y'all don't understand how important football is to Newton. These kids understand they have a responsibility when they step on the field for Newton. It's a special place to coach, Newton is. Everybody looks at us as a small place. We have a great school, great people, great fans, great parents. There is never a problem there. I've got the best job in the state of Texas. I've told people that. If somebody offered me $200,000 to go somewhere else, I wouldn't take it. I've got the best job. The people of

Newton have taken care of me when I went through my problems, and I can never repay 'em. I hope this helps a little bit. I can never give to them what they deserve. I love the people in Newton. There's a close bond between us ... and I am so happy for them."

Noah Williams was named the offensive MVP for the state title game. And the young man who had been injured for three consecutive seasons and had feared he might never get to play? Corbin Foster took home the defensive MVP trophy. Seeing his kids be rewarded for their perseverance was just part of the sacred beauty between the white lines for W.T. Johnston.

After the crush of interviews and press conferences, Johnston got to walk back out between those white lines to savor the moment. "Sometimes I imagine that after the final gun, I turned and looked into the stands. In my mind, I see a neatly dressed black man standing near the exit. He has a huge smile as he nods his head in satisfaction. And I can hear him saying to himself those words that got me through. 'Don't be afraid. I told you it would be all right.'

"Then I see him walking away. Just making his rounds."

Noah Williams and Corbin Foster hold MVP Awards after the Championship game.
(Courtesy of Newtonsports. com/Sherry Tracy)

Johnston leads a team prayer after
the Championship game.
(Courtesy of Newtonsports.com/
Sherry Tracy)

AFTERWORD

W.T. Johnston had etched his name alongside those of Lidney Thompson and Curtis Barbay. Newton celebrated with a parade on January 6, 2018. Because it is Newton, the citizens began to discuss the prospects for the next season. The consensus was that another parade could be possible. W.T. was not sure he would get to witness that if he were right about what was happening with his health.

On January 23, 2018, Johnston drove to Houston for an evaluation of his deteriorating lungs.

The tests were run, and the medical staff convened with Johnston. "I was prepared for the news to not be good. It wasn't. The doctors told me there was nothing else they could do. They estimated I had six to eight months to live."

In what had to be an awkward moment, W.T. pulled out gifts for his doctors. He had paid for championship rings for all of them. As Dr. Amit Parulekar, Dr. Goutham Dronavalli, and nurse practitioner Natalie Capuano opened their gifts, there were tears all around. As usual, W.T. had a word of comfort for others even as he received devastating news. "Something really good is going to come out of this. This whole experiment and what you learned is a part of God's plan."

Later he delivered a championship ring to Dr. Amin Alousi at MD Anderson.

"I told him I serve a really big God. I know how this is going to end up. I know where I am going. And they had learned a lot with this case that would help others."

Dr. Alousi had tears in his eyes as he responded. "I am glad you said that."

Johnston processed the diagnosis on his four-hour drive home. He called a couple of friends to share what the medical team said, still able to encourage and laugh with those closest to him.

He knew telling Debbie and the boys would be the hard part. He was not sure how that was going to work. The six-month time frame would end right before football camp began in August. He could not imagine not being a part of that annual rite.

That weekend, W.T. called the family together and shared the news, emphasizing how grateful he was for the "great gift" he had been given.

He was nearing the dreaded six-month deadline when God revealed another plan for Coach Johnston. Ennis coach Sam Harrell had been battling multiple sclerosis for years and had had to retire from coaching. After he received stem cell treatments in Panama, his disease was reversed, and he was actually returning to coach the Lions.

Could this treatment work for W.T.? Could he endure the journey to Panama? Did he even want to leave his family for a medical Hail Mary when time was so precious?

Then Johnston learned about another option. The state of Texas had passed legislation to allow stem cell treatments, but the procedures had not been finalized. W.T. did not have time for legislative foot-dragging. With help from his doctors, he prepared his case for the Texas attorney general. The state fast-tracked permission for W.T. to become a guinea pig one more time. No one knew if the treatments could help his rare diagnosis. You already know what his response was. "If it helps me, that would be great. But if me being a test case helps others, then it is worth it."

W.T. began stem cell treatments in San Antonio right before the start of fall football camp. "My first goal was to make it to August. I wanted the guys who built this team, those other coaches, to be the ones to finish the journey. I made it to August, and then I wanted to make it past the Gilmer game. I knew if we had problems, it would be in those first three tough games against Silsbee, West Orange, and Gilmer."

W.T. made it past Gilmer. He smiles as he shrugs his shoulders.

"After that, I was like, I might as well make it the rest of the way."

Again, the journey was rough. W.T. was back on oxygen full-time. His pain was relentless. But he was there between the white lines with his kids.

Newton was not able to put together a full schedule of games, and Johnston knew who to blame with his characteristic chuckle.

"Those announcers on Fox Southwest kept talking during the championship game about how many kids we were getting back for 2018 and how good Newton would be. Nobody wanted to play us after all that buildup."`

The Eagles made it through the regular season with a spotless record. The winning streak was now at twenty-six. Would God give W.T. Johnston another shot at a state championship? Who would have dreamed that the man given nine months in 2015, and then six to eight months in 2018, would be on the sideline for another shot? There was no other explanation for W.T. Johnston than the one he offered to the media.

"When the Lord is ready to take me is when I'm leaving—not before," Johnston said. "That's the way I run my life. Everything I base my life on is the Lord. Now, I think football 24-7, and I can't turn it off. I've always been that way. When they told me that news in March, it was

BETWEEN THE WHITE LINES

kind of surreal this time because I could see it happening, and I can see it happening now."

The Eagles made it to the semifinal game with no challenges.

That all changed when the East Bernard Brahmas met Newton in Porter, Texas. East Bernard played straight up with the Eagles and tied the score in the fourth quarter with a nine-minute scoring drive. Then they made one mistake. Even with the extended drive, East Bernard gave the ball to Josh Foster and the Eagles with two minutes left. Darwin Barlow punched it in from the one-yard line with thirteen seconds left on the clock. A sack of the Brahmas' quarterback sealed the deal.

Against all odds, W.T. would be on the sideline one more time for a state championship game. When he stood on the sideline at AT&T Stadium, he would mark three years, five months, and twenty-seven days since his original GvHD diagnosis. God had given W.T. a staggering 1,276 days so far to teach his kids and everyone around him how to live until you die.

He was so weak from preparing for the championship that the school administration arranged for him to travel to Arlington in an RV loaned from a local dealership. The media wasn't certain whether W.T. would be with his team on the sideline or in the press box for the game. Those people had not been following this man's story. Reporter Sarah Merrifield stopped by the locker room to greet Coach Johnston and noticed how tired he looked. She wondered if he could hold up under the strain ahead of him.

The opponent was the storied Canadian Wildcats, coached masterfully by Chris Koetting. For non-Texans, we should note that Canadian is located on the eastern side of the Texas Panhandle. The town was named after the Canadian River and not our northern neighbor. The Wildcats were a perennial power, and winning a back-to-back championship against this team would not be easy. W.T. Johnston did not want it any other way.

Once again his pregame speech was masterful. He had found a comment from a TV reporter about the lack of sophistication in the Eagle offense. The analyst had said that Newton's offense looked as if it were drawn up in the dirt compared to the sophisticated offense of their opponent. W.T. used that as a great motivator.

"That is what they think about us. That's insulting to y'all. Everything we do is coached out of precision. Show 'em. We are fixin' to get after them. They're pretty good, but we're pretty good too. Let's make 'em remember what?"

"The night they saw Newton!" the players shouted back.

"That's right! The night they saw Newton!"

The game looked as if it might be easier than expected when Newton jumped out to a 21–0 lead. But this Canadian team was too talented and too resilient to quit. The Wildcats climbed back in the second half and were able to slow down the Eagle attack. They were driving with a chance to win the game with less than a minute to go. A televised shot of W.T. Johnston sitting on his sideline chair showed him calm and confident.

On a fourth and eight play, quarterback Casen Cavalier lofted a pass into the end zone. Newton defender Dominique Seastrunk stepped in front of the receiver to intercept their last-ditch effort.

The cameras cut again to Johnston on the sideline when Josh Foster took the snap and knelt down in victory formation, sealing a 21–16 victory. The telecast captured the moment for W.T. as he clasped his hands in prayer and looked toward the heavens. He knew this was a special gift of grace.

His players lined up to hug their beloved coach. Drew Johnston embraced his dad. It was not lost on either of them that in January

W.T. Johnston thanks God for another State Title.
(Courtesy Newtonsports.com/ Sherry Tracy)

W.T. had been given no more than eight months to live. Eleven months later, he had guided his team to the first back-to-back championship in school history.

Reporter Sarah Merrifield knelt at Coach Johnston's side to get his thoughts just moments after the Eagles won.

"This has been a long journey. I can't even describe it. I'd have to have an hour to tell you," W.T. said. "We got together in August right before we started practicing, and I told them I probably wouldn't make it through the season. I was only given eight months to live. And I wanted them to be aware of what was going on. And then we got going, and there was about two or three weeks during the season I didn't think I was going to make it. And we talked about that.

"I always told them this was the last lesson I'm gonna teach them. I've been around these guys and their dads and their mothers since 1991. And I told them the last lesson I would ever teach them is how to live before you die, and where you put your strength and where you put your belief. The Lord has done so much for me. It's unbelievable what Jesus has let me do and see through these kids. And I tell everybody—they don't understand this—I've been given a great gift.... I've been able to see how my life could affect people before I die. These guys, they've touched my life. It's been a mutual thing. But I've been able to teach them a lesson that you don't get to see most times.

"Last night they were talking about wanting to win for me. This is their time. I've had my time ... . This is all for them. I told them, 'Do it for your teammates. Do it for you.' Because fifty years from now ...

they'll always remember this. This will be a special time. I mean, they'll remember me—if I've done right, a part of me is going to live in them, and that's what I've always thought—if I've done things right."

There is no doubt W.T. Johnston has done things right. Those postgame comments went viral, and more than three million people heard W.T. Johnston's testimony and story. When that was relayed to W.T., he knew what God had done.

"This is why He kept me alive for this game. Last year I didn't give Him enough credit. God gave me another chance. Once again, He has given me a great gift."

THE WHITE LINES

A personal word from W.T. Johnston to his coaching colleagues, written after he was diagnosed and given eight months to live

The white lines are the boundaries of the field in a football game. For me the white lines are a metaphor for dealing with life. The white lines are what I concentrate on when things are not going like I want them to. When things start happening at school like administrative problems and other things I have no control of, I let my mind go to the white lines. Now I am sitting at my desk planning for something six months from now, and I remember ... "T," you might not have six months. I still go to the white lines in my mind. What really matters, I think, are the white lines. I think if I take care of the white lines in the fall, everything else will take care of itself.

What is it going to take to be successful between the white lines? What kid can I make a difference in during the spring, summer, or two-a-days to help our team between the white lines? What kid can I instill confidence in, so that he can see self-worth in himself and, therefore, make a difference in our team? It's a shame, but I see kids all the time who I have more confidence in than they have in themselves.

The x's and o's are the easy part. Developing these kids is the hard and most important part of what we do. What drill, practice schedule, play, or defense can we add where both the team and I improve and have success between the white lines? I don't know about other coaches, but I think about this twelve months out of the year. I truly believe that there is nothing wrong with that. I have a fear of losing, and I don't think that's a bad thing either. I want to be around people who are not okay with losing and failure.

We all struggle with the white lines in our lives at some point. We struggle with things such as Am I doing enough to be successful? Am I good enough? How could I be worthy of God's love, mercy, and forgiveness? When things are not going like they should be in my life, why are these things happening? Why am I sick, why is my marriage in this shape, why am I a failure at my job? How can God love me even though I did some of the things in my life? How could He ever forgive me?

You would be surprised how many kids out there think they are not worthy or have done things so bad that the Lord could never forgive or love them. When you become a Christian, you inherit two things—an audience and an enemy. The audience is the people whom you surround yourself with or you come in contact with every day. They are watching you to see if you live the life you profess. The enemy is the prince of this world. He's telling you that you are bad and you are not worthy. He keeps telling you that God could never forgive you for what you've done and thought. He keeps saying, "Look at you, you're a mess."

I have learned that the white lines can be anything in your life that you choose for them to be. Your family, your job, your faith, anything that is important to you—something you choose. Sometimes we don't keep the white lines in the right perspective, and they control us too much. You are probably thinking I was just saying I can't turn it off. I did, but the white lines are where I can go to put things in perspective. To me they are what is important, so I slow down and quit worrying about things I can't control. The white lines should be a retreat, a place in our minds that we can go to simplify things in our lives and find the rest and peace we need. My white lines for years have been on Friday nights. They're my refuge, and I couldn't wait to get there.

The white lines are pure and simple. In the white lines there's no black, no white, no rich, no poor, and no political affiliation. The white lines are the great equalizer. Either you can or you can't. Pure competition, and the ones that have to think about it usually can't. Either you will compete or you won't. The white lines are the closest thing in sports to life. If you don't prepare, you fail. If you give in, you fail. If you panic, you fail. If you don't have discipline, you will not be successful.

Some of the greatest things about the white lines are the bonds and trust that come with competing as a team. To be successful in the white lines, you have to have trust that only comes from the struggles and successes with your teammates. When you've succeeded in the white lines as a team, there are bonds there that will never be broken. I've seen guys with more potential than one guy should have, but they won't compete. Additionally, I've seen guys who don't have as much potential, not as much athletic ability, but have something inside that you can't measure or see. The white lines expose both guys. The white lines are fair and don't lie.

There is another important meaning in my life for the white lines. This is where I go to find peace for my mind and soul. That's what I really want to come from this life I've got left and this book. The peace I have, I have found from my Lord Jesus Christ.

The white lines of a football field on Friday night are truly unbelievable in my mind. I still get the same feeling I did thirty years ago when I walked on the field for the first time. I think if you ever lose that feeling, it's time to get out. I don't think I'm going to live long enough to lose that feeling, and that bothers me.

The other night I sat by myself in the middle of the field at a track meet watching my kids compete. This was two days after my doctors told me I had only months left to live. During those moments, my mind went back to thirty years of the white lines. It was a special time, as I could remember games and plays I haven't thought of for years. I could remember and see kids I haven't thought about for years. I could see the joy, the happiness, the struggles, the jubilation, the pain, and all the preparation. I called Deb on the way home and told her I didn't realize how much I was gonna miss this. We won the track meet, but watching the kids perform in my mind from the past that night made me very sad that it was coming to an end.

To anyone reading this, don't take the white lines for granted! For my coaching friends, people would love to be where you are on Friday nights. I will miss the preparation and planning on Saturdays and Sundays, looking for a "W" Monday through Thursday and finding it on Friday! The smell of the grass and the sounds of the game, the camaraderie among the kids and coaches! I truly love it!! I will miss the white lines. My prayer is that you find the peace I have found between the white lines with Jesus.

W.T. JOHNSTON

AUTHOR'S NOTE

I had the privilege of spending a lot of time conversing with W.T. Johnston in person and on the phone over the past two years. I went to visit Coach on May 1, 2019, at his home in Newton. The plan was to go over some final details and questions about the book. When I got there, it was obvious W.T. was having a tough day physically. As always, he tried to be the gracious host but his breathing was labored. Even in that state he was able to clarify some facts in the book and discuss his beloved Texas Rangers. He talked about the future of the Newton Eagles and some great athletes who were coming through the system.

He gave me all he had that day but as the hours went by I knew he simply needed to rest. I told him I was heading home and asked if I could pray with him. He said yes and I knelt down and took W.T.'s hand. I prayed for peace and assurance of God's presence. My last words of that prayer would be my final words to my friend.

"And I pray that you will always keep your eyes on the Cross."

W.T.'s final word to me was a strong and confident "Amen".

W.T. Johnston died on May 11, 2019. I was honored to read a portion of his "White Lines" message during his memorial service at Singletary Field in Newton. I finished by reminding the hundreds in attendance of how my friend had kept his eyes on the Cross until the end.

"We are mistaken if we say we lost W.T. last weekend. The truth is, we know exactly where he is."

ACKNOWLEDGMENTS

I am so grateful to the Johnston family for allowing me to tell this story and for welcoming me into their circle.

I am especially grateful to Debbie Johnston. She has been a constant source of encouragement, information, and assistance in this project. W.T. may be one of the toughest people I have ever met but his wife should also be in that conversation. Without Debbie's assistance I am not sure this book could have happened.

Thanks to Drew and Kelsey Johnston for their contributions and kindness. I am grateful to Shaw Johnston for sharing his memories. Thanks to W.T.'s sister, Elizabeth Henderson, for providing family information.

I owe a debt of gratitude to Coach Greg Neece for his contributions to the football story and the special bond that W.T. shared with his brother Doug. Thanks to Jack Alvarez, Mike Tankersly, Curtis Hamilton, Lidney Thompson, and Kevin Gundy for their help.

I am grateful to Darwin Barlow and Corbin Foster for sharing their memories.

Thanks to Bobby Bean, Kristi Collins Staley, Lydia Jarrell Bean, and Tabor Westbrook for helping me understand and relate the unique charm and quiet strength of Newton, Texas. Thanks to Ed and Sherry Tracy of Newtonsports.com for graciously sharing from their wealth of photos.

Most of all, thank you to the special people of Newton who love the Eagles and loved Coach Johnston. You have welcomed me as one of your own and I will be forever grateful. I hope this book makes you proud about the amazing legacy of Coach Johnston and your special community.

Special Thanks ...

I would like to thank Bobby Bean and the Newton County Historical Commission for their assistance in providing research material. Mr. Bean's knowledge of Newton football proved invaluable in putting this story together. I am indebted to him and the NCHC for their wealth of historical background. If you would like to know more about this town and team I recommend Bobby Bean's book, *Once An Eagle...The History of Newton High School Football.*

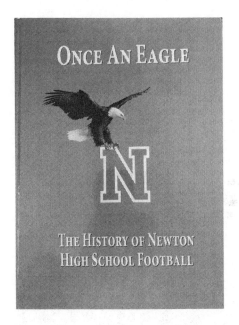

This beautiful hardcover book is $30. All proceeds go to The Newton County Historical Commission. **Books may be purchased through the History Center.**

To have a copy shipped to you, mail a check or money order for $30 + $6 shipping and handling to:

The Newton County Historical Commission
213 E. Court Street
Newton, Texas 75966

ABOUT THE AUTHOR

Dave Burchett is a successful television sports director with experiences that include the Olympic Games as well as professional and collegiate sports, earning a national Emmy and two local Emmys during his career. Dave directed television coverage of Texas Rangers baseball for thirty-seven consecutive years. He is the author of Waking Up Slowly: Spiritual Lessons from My Dog, My Kids, Critters, and Other Unexpected Places, Stay: Lessons My Dogs Taught Me about Life, Loss, and Grace; and When Bad Christians Happen to Good People. Dave and his wife, Joni, have three grown sons, six amazing grandchildren, and a rescued Lab.

A percentage of profits from the sale of *Between the White Lines* benefits the W.T. Johnston Scholarship Fund in Newton, Texas.

Made in the USA
Columbia, SC
30 April 2021

37131035R00112